FRESCO

by Scotto®

FRESCO

by Scotto®

Modern Tuscan Cooking for all Seasons

By Marion Scotto and Vincent Scotto

With contributions by Rosanna, Anthony, Jr., and Elaina Scotto

Photographs by Brian Hagiwara

Abbeville Press Publishers   New York   London   Paris

FRONT FLAP: *Seated:* Marion Scotto; *standing, left to right:* Rosanna, Elaina, Vincent, Anthony, Jr. BACK COVER: *Clockwise from left:* Focaccia with Robiola Cheese (recipe on page 88); Lemon Buttermilk Pound Cake with Mascarpone Whipped Cream (recipe on page 38); Grilled Pizza Margarita (recipe on page 165) and Grilled Pizza with Wild Mushrooms and Taleggio Cheese (recipe on page 163); Anthony Scotto, Jr.'s Bruschetta with Tomatoes (recipe on page 56) and Bistecca Fiorentina (recipe on page 71). FRONTISPIECE: Bread Salad with Grilled Shrimp (recipe on page 79).

EDITOR: Susan Costello
MANUSCRIPT EDITOR: Mary Goodbody
DESIGNER: Patricia Fabricant
TYPESETTER: Barbara Sturman
PRODUCTION EDITOR: Meredith Wolf
COPYEDITOR: Ginny Croft
PRODUCTION MANAGER: Lou Bilka

FOOD STYLIST: Dora Jonasson
PROP STYLIST: Christine McCabe

All photographs are by Brian Hagiwara except the following: Portrait (front flap), Andy Marcus; Fresco by Scotto® interior (page 15) and Potato and Zucchini Chips with Gorgonzola (page 173), Kenneth Chen; Spaghettini with Manila Clams, Olive Oil, Garlic, and Oven-Roasted Tomatoes (page 61), Richard Bowditch.

Whenever Fresco refers to the restaurant, the registered name is Fresco by Scotto®.

First edition
10 9 8 7 6 5 4 3 2 1

LIBRARY OF CONGRESS CATALOGING-IN-PUBLICATION DATA
Scotto, Marion.
    Fresco by Scotto : modern Tuscan cooking for all seasons / by Marion Scotto and Vincent Scotto, [with] Rosanna Scotto, Anthony Scotto, Jr., and Elaina Scotto; photographs by Brian Hagiwara.
       p. cm.
    Includes index.
    ISBN 0-7892-0294-8
    1. Cookery, Italian—Tuscan style. 2. Fresco by Scotto (Restaurant) I. Scotto, Vincent. II. Scotto, Rosanna. III. Scotto, Anthony. IV. Scotto, Elaina. V. Fresco by Scotto (Restaurant) VI. Title.
TX723.2.T86S26   1997
641.5945′5—dc20   96-44761

I would like to thank my husband, Anthony, who at first was concerned that this venture would not succeed, and now, is as proud of our success as we are.

Marion Scotto

ACKNOWLEDGMENTS

My love and very special thanks to the following people whose support and inspiration over the years have helped my career and made this book possible.

To my parents Mary and Vincent and my sister Donna, who tasted all my recipes, both successes and failures, and who constantly encouraged me.

To Marion, Anthony, Elaina, and Rosanna Scotto who took a chance naming me executive chef of Fresco by Scotto® and whom I consider to be extended family rather than employers.

To my sous chefs Robert Torio and Arlene Sadowski who helped test the recipes and who worked longer hours than usual to give me time to devote to the book.

To my friends and former employers whose knowledge and advice are always greatly appreciated: Leslie, Karl, and Rita Lofgren, Johanne Killeen and George Germon, Jeanne and Robie Fadel, MaryAnn and Christopher Walsh, Kyle Kelly, William Murphy, Eric Bell, Nataliya Gelman, Faith Heller Willinger, Diane and Cesare Benneli, Cindy and Ralph Brennan, Mary Goodbody, Deborah Callan, Karen Berman, Gerard Maras, and Arlene Wanderman.

Vincent Scotto

CONTENTS

SPRING

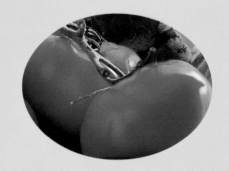

SUMMER

AUTUMN

Sandwiches

WINTER

Grilled Pizzas

PREFACE

When we opened our doors for the first time in November of 1993, we had only an inkling of what it meant to run a restaurant as busy as Fresco. The months leading up to that exciting day may have been fraught with disappointment, frustration, and hours of hard work, but as the saying goes, "If we'd known then what we know now . . . ," no doubt we would do it again!

We moved into our current location on East 52nd Street in the heart of Manhattan that summer and spent the next months knocking down walls, installing French doors at the front of the restaurant, and reconfiguring the dining and bar areas with the assistance of architect and designer Ted Moudis. We called on Bob Denning for his expertise when designing the private dining room.

As carpenters and electricians worked in the front of the house, we gathered in the kitchen—which is large by New York standards—with invited friends, such as Phyllis Cerf Wagner, to sample and critique the food Chef Vincent Scotto prepared. We did not expect our friends to be anything but brutally honest and fair. These were not dinner parties, they were business meetings. Fortunately, Vincent shared our standards of taste and quality, and so with few exceptions, we all ate extremely well during those months of trial and few errors. Tasting the wonderful food, working together to plan the decor, and seeing our dream physically take shape allowed us to believe that we might actually have a restaurant that worked. Happily, the past few years have proved us correct—many times over.

GETTING STARTED

When my son Anthony came home from California, where he had been running restaurants in Los Angeles and San Francisco, and told me he wanted to open a restaurant in New York, we never expected it to become a family venture. However, as we searched Manhattan from Chelsea to the Upper East Side, we realized how difficult finding a location would be. We also began to see that it would be more expensive than we had thought. Overall, this was a major undertaking. From talking to restaurateurs, I understood that Anthony's restaurant would have to become an endeavor involving the whole family. Not only did I happily get involved, but my daughter Elaina left her job in fashion to help out and my other daughter, Rosanna, who works in television news, devoted some spare time too.

Several times we believed our restaurant had found a home, only to discover a serious problem—after investing considerable time and money. We finally found our current location, but when we first met with the landlord, he had a hard time taking us seriously. "Go home and cook," he told me. I responded that while I might not have a track record, I knew that we, as a family, could create a wonderful restaurant. We persevered, and today our landlord, Burt Resnick, is nothing but supportive of Fresco.

A CHEF NAMED SCOTTO

We hired Stephen Kalt, one of the best restaurant consultants in the city, who proved invaluable in helping us pull together all the details, big and small, concerning opening the restaurant, not the least of which was finding a chef. While we were selecting silverware and searching for the blue glassware we knew we wanted, we launched this most important search.

Stephen placed an advertisement in *The New York Times,* using his own phone number. One day he told us a young man named Vincent was coming for an interview but neglected to tell us his last name. When Vincent walked in and we introduced ourselves, he admitted that his name was Scotto, too. Although we joked that the last thing we needed was "another Scotto around here," we had a feeling we had found our chef. When we discovered he was the same Vincent Scotto who had contributed to one of the cookbooks we had been reading all summer, with recipes we considered representative of the kind of food we hoped to serve, we hired him before he had even cooked for us! We took a chance hiring such a young chef (Vincent was only twenty-four), but it turned out to be one of our best decisions. Just six weeks after we opened, Ruth Reichl of *The New York Times* honored us with two stars. Soon Gael Greene of *New York Magazine,* Andy Birch from *Gourmet* magazine, and Bob Lape from Crain's *New York Business* were singing our praises too.

Vincent began by putting together a sample menu from the dishes we had offered to our friends during those early cozy kitchen meals. We barely altered this first menu on opening day, and many of the dishes have become signature ones, appearing on menu after menu, and some of these are included in this book.

A FAMILY BUSINESS

As a family, we travel to Italy once a year for a working vacation. Husbands, wives, and children all come along, and we move from restaurant to restaurant, sampling as many dishes as will fit on the table at one time, discussing each one, and taking copious notes. This is how we expand our menus and broaden our own knowledge. While our "discussions" may be spirited, we all share a love of good food and a vision for the restaurant, which is reflected in our business.

My daughter Elaina, who has a background in fashion, is wonderful at choosing accouterments for the restaurant and works on public relations. My daughter Rosanna, who works full-time as a news anchor on Fox Five television, spends many weekday hours at the restaurant, helping with promotion and working in the front of the restaurant during lunch. Anthony chooses the wines, hires the staff, and generally keeps the customers coming back for more. I handle all private parties, work on the menus with Vincent, and supervise the running of the restaurant.

Fresco means so much to all of us. Without question, it's a family business—there are never fewer than two of us there at any given time—and it's a passion. Before we opened, people who supported us (as well as the naysayers who thought we were in over our heads) asked us time and again about our "concept." We never liked the question, although the answer is simple.

Elaina researched the name, finally coming up with the word *fresco,* which we agreed conveyed our message of fresh food, the sort you might enjoy *al fresco,* or outdoors. But our name is not our concept. Nor is the modern Tuscan cuisine we serve (and strive daily and seasonally to improve upon). Plain and simple, our concept is making customers feel comfortable and welcome by serving delicious, fresh, seasonally inspired food. We have customers who come into the restaurant three or four times a week. Others come only once or twice a year. It doesn't matter. We try to make everyone welcome.

OUR CUSTOMERS

Being located in midtown Manhattan, we attract a variety of customers, including business men and women, politicians, and lots of television people. It helps that Rosanna has worked with celebrities such as Regis and Joy Philbin, who early on became two of our biggest supporters. Soon Kathie Lee Gifford came in with her husband, Frank, to be followed by Barbara Walters, Lynn Sherr, and Doug Johnson. Since we are located close to the NBC studios, we are often called their "commissary." Katie Couric, Matt Lauer, Al Roker, Bryant Gumbel, Sue Simmons, Ann Curry, Deborah Roberts, Chuck Scarborough, Jane Hanson, Mary Civiello, and Jim Watkins are frequent diners, as are Jack Cafferty, Kaity Tong, and Mr. G from WPIX-TV. Just about everyone Rosanna works with at Fox Five television is a faithful "regular," including John Roland, Penny Crone, Jim Ryan, and Lynn White. We've been honored to have actors such as Al Pacino, Tony Lo Bianco, Danny Aiello, Jennifer Aniston, William Baldwin, and Ed O'Neill join us for meals. One night actor Paul Sorvino stopped eating long enough to serenade a fellow customer with a rendition of "Happy Birthday to You"! Whitney Houston, Bobby Brown, Patti LaBelle, and Alanis Morissette have also eaten at Fresco. Politicians show up now and then as well. Brooklyn borough president Howard Golden, Bronx borough president Fernando Ferrer, Senator Al D'Amato, Mayor Rudolph Giuliani, and former mayors Ed Koch and David Dinkins have come back many times.

One winter's day Hillary Clinton was scheduled to make a fifteen-minute fundraising appearance at the restaurant. Earlier the same day at the Donahue show, the makeup man urged her to try our food, saying it was "the best in town." The First Lady took him at his word, and when she arrived, she asked Anthony if we could prepare dinner for her and her staff to take back on Air Force One. We were thrilled to do so.

OUR FUTURE

Above all, as the years go by, we hope to continue pleasing our loyal and enthusiastic customers. Soon, we are planning to open several small Frescos by Scotto, offering catering and take-out food. We take everything one step at a time, preferring to research and implement ideas ourselves.

We are enormously excited about this book. We hope it will satisfy the customers who frequently ask us for recipes. We also hope it will become a valued friend for the many home cooks who may never visit the restaurant but who appreciate good, flavorful Tuscan food made with the freshest and best ingredients. As a working family, we understand the constraints of so many other families to find time to prepare delicious, healthful meals. Many of our recipes are quick and easy, and even those that take a little time are not difficult. All are homey and unpretentious dishes we would not hesitate to prepare in our own homes, regardless of how casual or formal the occasion. We love this food and we are confident you will too.

From our family to yours: *buon appetito!*

—MARION SCOTTO

THE FRESCO KITCHEN

Welcome to our kitchen—a very American kitchen where dishes are prepared that originated in Tuscany. Bordering the Mediterranean Sea in northern Italy between Genoa and Rome, Tuscany is home to the glorious and ancient city of Florence, which today serves as the region's capital. Much of the food we serve at the restaurant and present on these pages has roots reaching back through the centuries and celebrating all that is wonderful about the cooking of Tuscany. We also offer a good selection of dishes that are quite modern, with American touches and flourishes not found in Italy. We embrace it all, taking what we love from both Tuscany and the United States, from the past and from the present. This is what we call modern Tuscan cooking.

Tuscany is a region widely admired for its rich traditions, both culinary and cultural. Here, the Italian language is thought to be purest—and the food the most simple and straightforward. Tuscans rely far more on fine, seasonal ingredients than they do on sauces and fancy techniques. The portions are generous and the flavors robust, earning Tuscany the reputation of having an unpretentious cuisine. Although it is characterized as pure and simple, it may also be regarded as the epitome of sophisticated cooking without any flashiness. Tuscans eat more beef than people do in other parts of Italy, and they also eat beans and rice (although not necessarily in the same dish, as the Spaniards do). In the towns strung along the seacoast, fish and seafood are prepared with finesse, with emphasis placed on the freshest catch of the day. And throughout the area, gardens and markets burst to overflowing

with tomatoes, peppers, zucchini, eggplant, fresh herbs, garlic, and onions—and cooks decide what to prepare based on the daily bounty.

We have adopted the culinary philosophy of Tuscany, relying on the freshest and best ingredients for preparation in our kitchen. In this book we offer many of our favorite and most popular recipes—all tested in a home kitchen so that you can easily prepare them in your own.

HOW WE COOK

Your kitchen will never be quite like ours. If you could spend just a short hour in the Fresco kitchen during a busy lunch or dinner time, you would quickly understand why. Six chefs work at the burners and grill; another five run the salad and cold appetizer station. A small band of pastry chefs create their own magic below stairs in our pastry kitchen. Chef Vincent Scotto positions himself just inside the kitchen door, where he can see the chefs and observe the wait staff as they carry plates in and out of the dining room at a brisk pace. He reviews the order slips and, with rapid-fire precision, instructs the cook at the appropriate station what to prepare, quickly summarizing any special requests or cooking advice. He times the preparations, encouraging a chef here, chiding another there, because his job is to make sure all orders are delivered to the table at the same time, hot and perfectly prepared.

At Fresco we don't cook much food ahead of time. One exception is our braised meats, which we feature on every menu and which by their very nature require long, slow, moist cooking. But as the orders arrive in the kitchen, we grill the chops and pizzas, cook the pasta, and sauté the fish. Our very name, which means "fresh" in Italian, demands this attention.

Anyone who has timed a meal so that every dish is ready at the same time will appreciate the challenge we meet daily. We in turn appreciate the challenge home cooks face. You may not feed hundreds of demanding New Yorkers every day, but you have to juggle children, jobs, shopping, and housekeeping while trying to get a good meal on the table. For those of you who, like us, appreciate full-flavored food made with the best ingredients possible, we have recipes to fit your busy lifestyle—quick and easy salads, pastas, grills, and sandwiches. We also have more time-consuming recipes that are just right for weekend parties and those days when you feel like spending time in the kitchen. As already mentioned, every recipe appearing in this book has been carefully tested in a home kitchen and, when appropriate, adapted for the home cook.

SEASONAL COOKING

Because we feel so strongly about using the freshest ingredients possible, we encourage our readers to do the same. The best way to do this is to cook and eat seasonally—as people have for generations in Tuscany. There, as here, in the days before refrigerated trucks and jet freight, people had no choice but to eat what was grown locally or could hold up to long, slow transport. Today markets carry fresh-looking raspberries in January and asparagus in November. While these foods are not bad, they are ever so much better when grown nearby and eaten soon after harvesting. Those wintertime raspberries are in season in Argentina or Chile in January—and therefore, unless you live in South America, will never

be as fresh as local ones in summer, which do not have to travel by jetliner to arrive in the store.

At the same time, we are not fanatics. We have arranged our recipes seasonally to encourage you to think in a certain way when you plan a meal, but we fully understand that there may be a chilly fall day when, for example, you want Crabmeat and Asparagus Lasagne or Arugula Pesto with Pennete. And why not? They are delightful dishes.

Several of our recipes—antipasti, bread salads, sandwiches, pizzas—have become signatures of the restaurant, particularly the bread salads and grilled pizzas. Depending on the ingredients used, they may be prepared at various times of the year. You will find them within the seasonal chapters. Many of our recipes are variations on the same theme, but none so much as these. Experiment with your own toppings for both the pizzas and the bread salads. Our recipes are only starting points intended to give you an understanding of our modern Tuscan style of cooking.

SELECTING AND STORING INGREDIENTS

Since all our recipes place great emphasis on fresh seasonal foods and simple preparations, we believe in buying the best you can afford, from the fruitiest extra-virgin olive oil to the ripest garden-grown tomato in the farmers market. Grow your own herbs and vegetables if possible, or rely heavily on those that are in season and sold at local farm stands. Buy fish and seafood from a fishmonger you trust and with whom you can develop a relationship. Establish the same kind of relationship with a good butcher. Make a trip to a nearby specialty store or Italian market now and then and stock your pantry with vinegars, dried mushrooms, Italian medium-grain rice, and a variety of dried pastas. Watch for Italian cheeses, buying the best imported brands you can find. This extra effort will make a noticeable difference in your cooking.

Whether you are buying fresh produce from the green market or selecting fresh fish or a certain cut of meat, there are some general guidelines that will make the task more successful. We rely on our suppliers and the expert eye of our chef to ensure that the food we serve at Fresco is the best there is. You must rely on your own instincts and knowledge—often during a hectic shopping trip sandwiched between your other daily chores. But regardless of how harried you are, take a few minutes to select the best and the freshest.

Vegetables and Fruit

Shop seasonally and locally whenever possible. A crop of tomatoes or peaches that has been grown and picked nearby will most likely be fresher than one harvested on the other side of the country and trucked into your region. Following this advice, shop at local green markets, farm markets, and roadside stands. Get to know the vendors and, when possible, the farmers. Ask what is freshest and best—and be flexible enough to alter your menu on the spot to include, say, zucchini rather than broccoli, leeks rather than shallots, or red leaf rather than Bibb lettuce.

This practice does limit you, however, to buying vegetables and fruits only in season and drastically narrows your choices. Many supermarkets and specialty shops sell wonderful, sometimes exotic produce all year long. Pineapples flown in from Hawaii the day after their harvest are a better buy than pineapples from Central America that have traveled in crates in the cargo holds of ships—although the Hawaiian fruit will

be more expensive. Apply this to buying other fruits and vegetables not native to your region or to the season. It is poor economics to try to save money with cut-rate limp green beans or mealy apples. Weigh freshness against price—and freshness should win every time.

When selecting vegetables and fruit, look for those that have good color, firm configuration, and a fresh, clean aroma. (But don't let visual perfection be your guide. Organically raised produce is often less than perfect in form and shape—but tastes terrific.) Some produce, such as peaches and strawberries, has a noticeable and pleasing aroma. Other produce should smell of nothing more than the sun and the earth. Avoid old-looking produce with browned leaves, too many soft spots, or wrinkled skin. Gently prod and squeeze fruits and melons, taking care not to bruise them. Pick up melons to gauge their heft (heavy is good) and apples their firmness. Avoid fruits that are very underripe (green) or on the verge of being overripe.

In most cases, vegetables are at their peak of freshness and flavor the moment they are harvested. Good suppliers know this and take advantage of jet transport and sensible refrigeration to keep their products flavorful and appealing. You should follow their example and refrigerate vegetables as soon as you bring them home. But don't count on the refrigerator to keep them fresh for long; try to eat them within a day or two of purchase. Exceptions include tomatoes, potatoes, and dry-skinned onions, none of which should be refrigerated.

Fruit is often picked unripe and then allowed to ripen at room temperature. If you buy unripe fruit (firm peaches or plums, hard pears, unyielding cantaloupes), let it sit out rather than refrigerating it. Once it is ripe, put the fruit in the refrigerator—or better yet, eat it right away. Apples do not ripen sitting out on the kitchen counter and so should be bought fully ripe, crisp, and juicy. Always store cherries, berries, and grapes in the refrigerator. When handling tropical fruits such as citrus and mangoes, keep their warm homeland in mind and don't refrigerate them unless you have to.

Poultry and Meat

The best way to ensure that the poultry and meat you buy are the best available is to establish a good relationship with a reputable butcher. As supermarkets increasingly supplant small local businesses, however, independent butchers are becoming difficult to find. Fortunately, many supermarket meat departments have butchers on staff who can answer questions and become valuable allies.

Free-range chickens and turkeys—birds that are raised in open pens and allowed to scratch for their food, which is scattered on the ground—are the best choices. They taste better and richer and have less fat. They are also more expensive than mass-produced poultry. Whichever you choose, be sure the poultry does not smell anything but fresh and that the skin and flesh are firm, evenly colored, and smooth. Store poultry in the coolest part of the refrigerator (in most home refrigerators this is the back of the lowest shelf), and eat it within a day or two of purchase. If you plan to freeze the poultry, wrap it well in plastic (cling film) and foil and freeze it for no longer than two months.

Rinse all poultry and trim any noticeable fat before cooking. To eliminate the chance of salmonella, wash all surfaces used while preparing the poultry, the knives, and your hands with warm soapy water and keep other foods separate from the raw poultry.

Beef, veal, pork, and lamb are most tender and tasty when young and the flesh is markedly firm and smooth. High-quality beef has bright red meat and pure white marbling. Current tastes dictate that beef not have as much marbling (fat) as it used to, although some marbling ensures moist meat. The bones should look white, firm, and flat—not crumbly.

Aged beef is quite expensive and generally hard to find except at very fine butcher shops. Only high-quality cuts from young animals are aged. The process involves hanging the meat for two to eight weeks in a controlled environment with a very low temperature (just above freezing) so that its flavor and texture change slightly, making the beef taste better to some connoisseurs. Most aged meat is available only to the restaurant trade, so do not be surprised if you cannot find it.

Veal, which, of course, is young beef, has virtually no fat or marbling and very mild flavor. Look for pale pink meat. Very young veal may be milk-fed, which means it will be very pale, almost white, and even more tender and milder than older veal.

Pork should be young, lean, and pink in color, with soft, pink-tinged bones. Some cuts are covered with pure white fat, which is acceptable. Avoid older, darker red pork with brittle white bones.

When buying lamb, look for clear, pink meat; soft, moist, pinkish-white bones; and pure white fat, although young lamb has very little, if any, marbling. The best legs of lamb weigh about 5 pounds (2.25 kg) —a leg heavier than 9 pounds (4 kg) indicates an older, less desirable animal. The best lamb chops, too, are small—and very expensive.

Refrigerate all meat as soon as possible, storing it (like poultry) in the coldest section of the refrigerator. Trim excess fat from the meat before cooking. If you plan to freeze the meat, wrap it well in plastic (cling film) and foil and eat it within a couple of months.

Fish and Seafood

As with meat and poultry, finding a reliable vendor is one of the best ways to guarantee you get the best fish and seafood. Regardless of where you buy fish, however, freshness is key. Frozen fish tastes cottony and dry and has very little flavor. Avoid it at all costs.

Fresh fish has a noticeable fresh scent. If it is an ocean fish, it smells slightly of the sea. It *never* smells "fishy," and for this reason, the fish store should not smell fishy either, but cool, fresh, and slightly salty. The gills on fresh fish are clean and rosy red, the eyes clear and protruding (with some exceptions), and the scales flat against the fish. Whole fish should be slightly stiff —not limp. Whether whole or filleted, the fish's flesh should be firm and smooth. Fish fillets and steaks should look moist and somewhat translucent—never bruised, opaque, or grainy.

Shellfish and crustaceans are best when still in the shell—although at times it is more expedient to buy shrimp and lobster meat out of the shell. Bivalves such as clams and oysters should be tightly closed, although mussels and some soft-shell clams may gape a tiny bit. Scallops are nearly always sold out of the shell and should be shiny white, with no odor. If possible, buy live lobsters and crabs that are noticeably moving about in the tank.

Always keep fish and shellfish cold. Buy it last when shopping, and the minute you get home, rinse it off, wrap it in clean paper, and store it in the coldest section of the refrigerator. It's a good idea to keep the wrapped fish in a colander set over a dish of ice cubes in the refrigerator. This keeps the fish extra cold, and the colander separates it from any water from melting ice. Store shellfish in the refrigerator covered with a damp kitchen towel. Oysters should always be stored flat—not jumbled in a bowl—to keep their brine inside the shells.

Fresco by Scotto®

SPRING

Considering that the literal translation of this title is "cooked water," it's not surprising that this is a very simple soup—a poor man's soup. The ingredient list is long, but all are modest foods (vegetables and fresh herbs) that are found in every kitchen garden in Tuscany. It's the addition of the poached egg that makes this a meal.

(photograph on page 17)

Acqua Cotta

½ pound (230 g) kale leaves
¼ cup (60 ml) olive oil
2 cups (230 g) finely diced onions
2 cups (230 g) finely diced carrots
1 cup (115 g) finely diced fennel (about 1 medium bulb)
2 tablespoons chopped garlic
1 to 2 teaspoons crushed red pepper flakes, or to taste
1 tablespoon chopped fresh sage
1 teaspoon chopped fresh rosemary
3 tablespoons chopped fresh flat-leaf parsley
1½ pounds (675 g) plum (egg) tomatoes, peeled, seeded, and chopped (about 3 cups)
1 cup (230 g) julienned Roasted Red Peppers (page 168)
Kosher salt to taste
6 slices Tuscan Bread (page 173) or other peasant-style bread
1 or 2 whole cloves garlic
6 large eggs
2 tablespoons extra-virgin olive oil
½ cup (55 g) freshly grated Parmesan cheese

1. In a large pot of boiling water, blanch the kale for about 1 minute, until barely wilted. Using a slotted spoon, transfer the kale to a bowl of cold water to stop the cooking and then immediately lift it from the water, shake off the excess water, and transfer to a plate. Set aside.

2. In a large stockpot, heat the ¼ cup (60 ml) of oil over medium heat. Add the onions, carrots, fennel, garlic, red pepper flakes, sage, rosemary, and parsley and cook, stirring frequently, for 20 to 25 minutes, or until the vegetables soften.

3. Add the tomatoes and cook for 15 to 20 minutes longer, until the tomatoes are so soft they fall apart. Add 5 cups (1.2 l) of water, the kale, and the red peppers, bring to a simmer over medium-high heat, and cook for about 20 minutes. Season to taste with salt.

Pages 16–17, left to right: Spaghettini with Olive Oil, Garlic, Zucchini, and Zucchini Blossoms (recipe on page 28); Acqua Cotta

4. Meanwhile, toast the bread until lightly browned and then rub the slices with the whole garlic cloves. Put a slice of toast in each of 6 serving bowls.

5. Reduce the heat to medium, so that the liquid is gently simmering. Carefully crack 1 egg into a cup, keeping the yolk whole. Slide the egg into the simmering liquid. Repeat with the remaining eggs, cooking each egg for 2 to 3 minutes, until poached.

6. As it poaches, lift each egg from the pot and position it on a piece of toast. Ladle some of the hot broth and vegetables over each. Drizzle each with 1 teaspoon of the extra-virgin olive oil and garnish with grated cheese.

SERVES 6

Note: To make it easier to poach the eggs, remove some vegetables from the pot before adding the eggs. Return the vegetables to the pot and heat them through before spooning them over the eggs. The soup can be made 2 days in advance without the eggs. Just before serving, poach the eggs. Serve as directed.

Onion-Roasted Garlic Soup with Fontina Croutons

> *3 tablespoons (45 ml) olive oil*
> *3 tablespoons (45 g) unsalted butter*
> *6 pounds (2.7 kg) onions, cut in julienne*
> *1 cup (230 g) Roasted Garlic (page 168)*
> *2 quarts (2 l) Chicken Stock (page 171)*
> *2 tablespoons fresh thyme leaves*
> *Salt and freshly ground black pepper to taste*
> *Fontina Croutons (recipe follows)*

1. Divide the oil and butter between 2 large, heavy-bottomed pans, and heat over medium heat until the butter melts. Add half the onions to each pan and cook, covered, stirring often, for 30 to 45 minutes, or until very soft, light amber in color, and caramelized. Combine the onions in one pan.

This soup is our version of French onion soup—with some notable changes. We lighten it by using chicken stock rather than the traditional veal stock, and we add fresh thyme, a mild herb that complements the onions and garlic. We also use lots of roasted garlic for deep, rich flavor. Be sure to let the onions caramelize and turn amber; otherwise their flavor will not be as intensely sweet and wonderful.

(continued on page 20)

2. In a small bowl, mash the roasted garlic.

3. Add the garlic, stock, and thyme to the onions and season to taste with salt and pepper. Reduce heat to low and simmer for 45 minutes, until the flavors blend.

4. Adjust the seasoning with salt and pepper. Float croutons on the top of each bowl of soup.

SERVES 6 TO 8

Fontina Croutons

> *4 cups (180 g) fresh bread cubes (1½- to 2-inch/4- to 5-cm cubes)*
> *¼ cup (60 g) unsalted butter, melted*
> *5 ounces (140 g) fontina cheese, shredded (about 1½ cups)*

1. Preheat the oven to 350°F (175°C).

2. Place the cubed bread in a large bowl. Drizzle with the butter and toss. Add the cheese and toss to distribute evenly.

3. Spread the croutons on a nonstick baking sheet in a single layer. (Or on a regular baking sheet lined with parchment paper.) Bake for 15 to 20 minutes, or until the croutons are golden brown. Remove from the oven and let cool on the baking sheet. Break into pieces and serve.

MAKES ABOUT 4 CUPS

Note: *The nonstick surface or the parchment paper prevents the croutons from sticking. Don't rely on an oiled baking sheet alone—the croutons may stick and be difficult to lift from the sheet. During baking, the cheese will melt and the croutons will resemble a solid mass, but when they cool, they can be broken into individual pieces. The cheese softens upon contact with the hot soup.*

We serve these floating on top of the Roasted Garlic Soup, scattered over vegetable soups, on top of stews, and even tossed into salads. Fontina is the best cheese to use because it melts to a smooth, silken mass. For delicious croutons use fresh bread cubes made from chewy peasant-style Italian bread or Tuscan Bread (page 173).

Fresh Pea Soup

½ cup (120 ml) olive oil
2 cups (260 g) diced onions
1½ cups (170 g) diced carrots
1 cup (115 g) diced fennel
2 tablespoons chopped garlic
1 teaspoon crushed red pepper flakes, or to taste
6 cups (1.5 l) Chicken Stock (page 171)
4 cups (565 g) fresh or frozen peas (1¼ pounds shelled peas)
1½ cups (215 g) diced potatoes
2 tablespoons chopped fresh flat-leaf parsley

1. In a large pot, heat the oil over medium heat. Add the onions, carrots, fennel, garlic, and red pepper flakes and cook, stirring occasionally, for about 15 minutes, until tender.

2. In another pot, heat the stock over high heat until boiling. Add half of the peas and blanch for about 4 minutes. Reserve about ¾ cup (180 ml) of the stock and strain the rest into the pot with the vegetables. Transfer the blanched peas to a food processor fitted with the metal blade and process until smooth. Add as much of the reserved stock as necessary for a smooth puree. You may not need all of it. (Add what you do not use to the pot with the vegetables.) Transfer the pureed peas to the pot with the vegetables.

3. Add the potatoes and cook over medium-high heat for 12 to 15 minutes, until the potatoes are tender. Add the remaining peas and the parsley, season to taste with salt, and heat through.

SERVES 6

Note: For a heartier soup, add 4 ounces (125 g) of julienned prosciutto to the vegetables in step 1. The soup can be prepared through step 2 and refrigerated, covered, for up to 2 days.

Although we have rarely encountered pea soup in Italy, Vincent has always loved it, especially in the spring, when peas are fresh and tender. This explains why we decided to serve it at Fresco, where we add lots of garlic and red pepper flakes. It's an easy soup with a nice, simple fresh flavor.

Bucatini with Crab Sauce

½ cup (120 ml) olive oil
12 blue crabs, backs removed, rinsed and patted dry (about
   2 pounds/900 g)
2 tablespoons chopped garlic
1½ cups (375 ml) dry white wine
8 cups (2 l) tomato puree
1 teaspoon crushed red pepper flakes, or to taste
3 tablespoons chopped fresh basil
Salt to taste
1½ pounds (675 g) bucatini or spaghetti (see Note)

1. In a large stockpot, heat 6 tablespoons of oil over medium heat. Add 6 crabs and sauté, uncovered, for 2 to 3 minutes, until the shells turn orange. Turn each crab a few times during cooking. Transfer the crabs to a plate and set aside. Add the remaining oil if necessary, sauté the remaining crabs, and set aside.

2. Add the garlic to the pot and sauté for about 1 minute, until softened. Reduce the heat to medium-low and return the crabs to the pot. Add the wine, tomato puree, red pepper flakes, and basil and simmer, partially covered, for about 2 hours to give the sauce time to develop its flavor.

3. In a large pot of lightly salted boiling water, cook the pasta for 6 to 8 minutes, until al dente. Drain, reserving 1 cup (250 ml) of the cooking water.

4. Add the pasta to the sauce and cook for 1½ to 2 minutes, tossing gently to coat the pasta with sauce. If the sauce is too thick, add some of the reserved cooking water.

5. Transfer the pasta to a serving platter, arranging the whole crabs on top. Serve immediately.

SERVES 6

Note: Bucatini is hollow strand pasta (similar to a drinking straw). It is also called perciatelli.

Crabmeat and Asparagus Lasagne

BÉCHAMEL SAUCE
3 cups (750 ml) milk
1 shallot, coarsely chopped
¼ teaspoon freshly grated nutmeg
4½ tablespoons (70 g) unsalted butter
4½ tablespoons (40 g) unbleached all-purpose (plain) flour
Salt to taste

LASAGNE
3 tablespoons (45 g) unsalted butter
3 tablespoons (45 ml) olive oil
4 cups (450 g) julienned onions (about 1 pound)
Salt and freshly ground black pepper to taste
6 cups (675 g) julienned asparagus (about 1½ pounds)
½ pound (230 g) prosciutto, finely chopped
2 cups (230 g) diced fresh mozzarella cheese
1 cup (230 g) fresh ricotta cheese
3 cups (340 g) freshly grated Parmesan cheese (about ¾ pound)
2 large eggs
¼ cup (10 g) chopped fresh flat-leaf parsley
1 pound (450 g) fresh pasta sheets or 8 ounces (230 g) dried lasagne sheets
½ cup (120 ml) heavy (double) cream
1½ pounds (675 g) lump crabmeat, well drained (about 4 cups)

1. To make the béchamel sauce, combine 2½ cups (630 ml) of the milk, the shallot, and nutmeg in a small saucepan and bring to a boil over medium heat. Reduce the heat and simmer, uncovered, for about 5 minutes. Cover and set aside to keep hot.

2. In another saucepan, melt the butter over medium-low heat. Add the flour and, using a wooden spoon, stir until the flour absorbs the butter and forms a roux. Continue stirring for 2 to 3 minutes longer while the mixture bubbles and thickens.

3. Slowly pour the hot milk into the flour, whisking continuously to prevent lumps. Bring the sauce to a boil over medium heat. Reduce the heat and simmer for 2 to 3 minutes, until smooth and thickened. Season to taste with salt.

4. Strain through a fine sieve into a bowl or glass measuring cup. Add as much of the remaining ½ cup (120 ml) milk as necessary to make 2½ cups (630 ml), whisking well to incorporate. Set aside, covered, until ready to use (see Note).

5. To prepare the lasagne, in a large skillet, heat the butter and olive oil over medium heat until the butter melts. Add the onions and cook, stirring often, for 25 to 30 minutes, until softened and beginning to caramelize. Season to taste with salt and set aside until ready to use.

6. Bring a pot of water to a boil, add the asparagus, and cook for about 4 minutes, until slightly softened. Drain and set aside to cool.

7. In a small bowl, combine the prosciutto, mozzarella, ricotta, 2 cups (230 g) of Parmesan, the eggs, and parsley. Stir well and season to taste with salt and pepper.

8. If using dried lasagne, bring a large pot of lightly salted water to a boil and cook the pasta for 8 to 10 minutes, until barely al dente. Drain and separate the sheets to cool. If using fresh pasta, do not cook it before assembling the lasagne.

9. Preheat the oven to 350°F (175°C).

10. In a 9 × 13-inch (23 × 33-cm) baking pan that is at least 2 inches (5 cm) deep, spread the cream over the bottom, tilting the pan if necessary to spread evenly. Lay a quarter of the pasta sheets over the cream, overlapping slightly and trimming if necessary to fit.

11. Spread a third of the cheese mixture evenly over the pasta. Top with a third of the onions, a third of the asparagus, and a third of the crabmeat. Drizzle ¾ cup (180 ml) of the béchamel sauce over the crabmeat. Top with more pasta sheets. Repeat layering with a third of the cheese, onions, asparagus, and crabmeat and ¾ cup béchamel sauce. Repeat the process, ending with pasta sheets on top. Press down to compress the layers slightly. Pour the remaining béchamel sauce evenly over the pasta and sprinkle with the remaining 1 cup (110 g) of Parmesan.

12. Bake, uncovered, for about 1 hour, until the top is golden brown and the sides are bubbling. Let stand 10 to 15 minutes before serving.

SERVES 6 TO 8

Note: The béchamel sauce, onions, asparagus, cheese mixture, and crabmeat filling can be prepared and refrigerated, covered, up to 2 days in advance. Before using the chilled béchamel, thin it slightly by whisking in 3 to 4 tablespoons (50 to 60 ml) of milk if necessary.

Here's another lasagne that is a play on traditional Tuscan cooking. The Italians don't cook with corn (maize) the way we do, but we're convinced that if they had access to sweet corn as good as ours, they would use it liberally. This is a dish that spans the spring-into-summer season: make it with fresh asparagus in the spring, and when summer arrives, take advantage of fresh sweet corn.

Lasagne with Corn, Asparagus, and Roasted Peppers

BÉCHAMEL SAUCE
3 cups (750 ml) milk
1 shallot, coarsely chopped
¼ teaspoon freshly grated nutmeg
4½ tablespoons (70 g) unsalted butter
4½ tablespoons (40 g) unbleached all-purpose (plain) flour
Salt to taste

LASAGNE
3 tablespoons (45 g) unsalted butter
3 tablespoons (45 ml) olive oil
4 cups (450 g) julienned onions (about 1 pound)
6 cups (675 g) julienned asparagus (about 1½ pounds)
3 cups (340 g) fresh or frozen corn kernels (5 to 6 ears)
2 cups (450 g) julienned Roasted Red Peppers (page 168)
Salt and freshly ground black pepper to taste
2 cups (230 g) diced fresh mozzarella cheese
1 cup (230 g) fresh ricotta cheese
3 cups (340 g) freshly grated Parmesan cheese (about ¾ pound)
2 large eggs
¼ cup (10 g) chopped fresh flat-leaf parsley
1 pound (450 g) fresh pasta sheets or 8 ounces (230 g) dried lasagne sheets
½ cup (120 ml) heavy (double) cream

1. To make the béchamel sauce, combine 2½ cups (630 ml) of the milk, the shallot, and nutmeg in a small saucepan and bring to a boil over medium heat. Reduce the heat and simmer, uncovered, for about 5 minutes. Cover and set aside to keep hot.

2. In another saucepan, melt the butter over medium-low heat. Add the flour and, using a wooden spoon, stir until the flour absorbs the butter and forms a roux. Continue stirring for 2 to 3 minutes longer while the mixture bubbles and thickens.

3. Slowly pour the hot milk into the flour, whisking continuously to prevent lumps. Bring the sauce to a boil over medium heat. Reduce the heat and simmer for 2 to 3 minutes, until smooth and thickened. Season to taste with salt.

4. Strain through a fine sieve into a bowl or glass measuring cup. Add as much of the remaining ½ cup (120 ml) milk as necessary to make 2½ cups (630 ml), whisking well to incorporate. Set aside, covered, until ready to use (see Note).

5. To prepare the lasagne, in a large skillet, heat the butter and olive oil over medium heat until the butter melts. Add the onions and cook, stirring often, for 25 to 30 minutes, until softened and beginning to caramelize. Season to taste with salt and set aside until ready to use.

6. Bring a pot of water to a boil, add the asparagus, and cook for about 4 minutes, until slightly softened. Using a slotted spoon, remove the asparagus from the pot and set aside to cool. Return the water to a boil, add the corn, and cook for 2 to 3 minutes, until softened. Drain and set aside to cool separately from the asparagus. Season the asparagus, corn, and roasted red peppers to taste with salt and pepper.

7. In a bowl, combine the mozzarella, ricotta, 2 cups (230 g) of the Parmesan, the eggs, and parsley. Stir well and season to taste with salt and pepper.

8. If using dried lasagne, bring a large pot of lightly salted water to a boil and cook the pasta for 8 to 10 minutes, until barely al dente. Drain and separate the sheets to cool. If using fresh pasta, do not cook it before assembling the lasagne.

9. Preheat the oven to 350°F (175°C).

10. In a 9 × 13-inch (23 × 33-cm) baking pan that is at least 2 inches (5 cm) deep, spread the cream over the bottom, tilting the pan if necessary to spread evenly. Lay a quarter of the pasta sheets over the cream, overlapping slightly and trimming if necessary to fit.

11. Spread a third of the cheese mixture evenly over the pasta. Top with a third of the onions, a third of the peppers, a third of the asparagus, and a third of the corn. Drizzle ¾ cup (180 ml) of the béchamel sauce over the corn. Top with a quarter of the pasta sheets. Repeat layering with a third of the cheese, onions, peppers, asparagus, and corn and ¾ cup béchamel sauce. Repeat the process, ending with the pasta sheets. Press down to compress the layers

(continued on page 28)

slightly. Pour the remaining béchamel sauce evenly over the pasta and sprinkle with the remaining 1 cup (110 g) of Parmesan.

12. Bake, uncovered, for about 1 hour, until the top is golden brown and the sides are bubbling. Let stand 10 to 15 minutes before serving.

SERVES 6 TO 8

Note: The béchamel sauce, onions, peppers, asparagus, corn, and cheese mixture can be prepared and refrigerated, covered, up to 2 days in advance. Before using the chilled béchamel, thin it slightly by whisking in 3 to 4 tablespoons (50 to 60 ml) of milk if necessary.

Spaghettini with Olive Oil, Garlic, Zucchini, and Zucchini Blossoms

What is so wonderfully Italian about this dish is its utter simplicity. The blossoms of the zucchini (courgettes) provide a delightful perfume, and the squash itself has a light, fresh flavor. In Italy this is a typical spring dish when zucchini are in bloom.

(photograph on page 16)

> 4¾ cups (1.18 l) olive oil
> 1½ pounds (675 g) zucchini (courgettes), seeded and diced (about ¾ cup; see Note)
> 1½ pounds (675 g) spaghettini or thin spaghetti
> 1 tablespoon coarsely chopped garlic
> 1½ teaspoons crushed red pepper flakes
> 5 fresh zucchini blossoms, roughly chopped (see Note)
> ⅓ cup (15 g) chopped fresh flat-leaf parsley, plus more for garnish
> Salt to taste
> 6 to 8 whole fresh zucchini blossoms, for garnish

1. In a large pot or deep skillet, heat 4 cups (1 l) of the oil (or enough oil for a depth of 2 inches/5 cm) over medium-high heat until very hot and nearly smoking. Fry a third of the zucchini for 4 to 5 minutes, until golden. Using a slotted spoon, lift the zucchini from the oil and set aside to drain on several layers of paper towels (kitchen paper). Repeat with the remaining zucchini, frying it in 2 or 3 more batches.

2. In a large pot of lightly salted water, cook the pasta for 4 to 6 minutes, until barely al dente. Drain, reserving 2 cups (500 ml) of the cooking water, and set aside.

3. In a large sauté pan, heat the remaining ¾ cup (180 ml) of oil over medium-high heat and sauté the garlic and red pepper flakes for about 30 seconds, until softened but not browned.

4. Add the pasta and 1½ cups (375 ml) of the reserved pasta cooking water to the pan and toss to coat with the oil and garlic. Raise the heat to high and cook for 6 to 8 minutes, tossing, until the pasta is tender and the liquid has evaporated. Add the remaining cooking water if necessary to cook the pasta.

5. Add the fried zucchini, chopped zucchini blossoms, and parsley and toss for 1 to 2 minutes, just until the blossoms wilt and the ingredients are well mixed. Season to taste with salt. Serve immediately, garnished with the whole zucchini blossoms and parsley.

SERVES 6

Note: If the zucchini are less than ½ inch (1.3 cm) in diameter, they do not need to be seeded. Zucchini blossoms are edible flowers available from farmer's markets and Italian markets in the late spring and early summer. While this pasta can be made without them, they add delicate flavor and pretty color. You can substitute nasturtiums, another edible flower.

Pappardelle with Chicken and Spinach

½ cup plus 2 tablespoons (150 ml) olive oil
1 pound (450 g) fresh spinach, trimmed and torn or chopped coarsely
4 cups (1 l) Chicken Stock (page 171)
4 teaspoons coarsely chopped garlic
1 teaspoon crushed red pepper flakes, or to taste
2¼ cups (565 g) canned crushed tomatoes
½ cup (20 g) chopped fresh basil
¼ cup (10 g) chopped fresh flat-leaf parsley
3 cups (500 g) shredded roasted chicken
Kosher salt to taste
1½ pounds (675 g) pappardelle or other wide noodles
   (see Note)

We make this with roasted chicken to take advantage of both light and dark meat, but it can be made with chicken cutlets as well. It's a lovely recipe to serve for a simple meal because it includes both meat and vegetables. Try to use a rich homemade chicken stock for the best flavor.

(continued on page 30)

Pappardelle with
Chicken and Spinach
(continued from page 29)

4 tablespoons (60 g) unsalted butter
1 cup (115 g) freshly grated Parmesan cheese

1. In a large skillet, heat 2 tablespoons of the oil over medium heat. Add the spinach and cook, uncovered, for 2 to 3 minutes, until the spinach is wilted. Drain and set aside. You may have to do this in batches.

2. In a large saucepan, simmer the stock over medium-high heat, uncovered, for 5 to 7 minutes, until it reduces by half.

3. In a large stockpot, heat the remaining ½ cup (120 ml) of oil over medium-low heat and cook the garlic for about 1 minute, until golden brown. Add the red pepper flakes, tomatoes, reduced stock, basil, and parsley. Raise the heat, bring to a simmer, and cook for 15 minutes. Add the chicken and cook 5 minutes longer, until the chicken is heated through. Season to taste with salt.

4. Bring a large pot of lightly salted water to a boil and cook the pasta for 6 to 8 minutes, until barely al dente. Drain, reserving ½ cup (120 ml) of the cooking water.

5. Add the spinach, butter, and pasta to the sauce and cook over high heat for 1 to 2 minutes, until blended. If the pasta seems dry, add some of the reserved cooking water and toss gently.

6. Divide the pasta evenly among 6 bowls and ladle extra sauce on top of each. Garnish generously with Parmesan and serve hot.

SERVES 6

Note: Pappardelle noodles are about 1 inch (2.5 cm) wide.

Risotto with Shrimp, Arugula, and Lemon

2½ cups (625 ml) clam juice
6 tablespoons (90 ml) pure olive oil
5 whole cloves garlic
2 cups (280 g) arborio or carnaroli rice
⅓ cup (80 ml) dry white wine

½ pound (230 g) uncooked shrimp (prawns), peeled, deveined, and
*   cut into ⅓-inch (8-mm) pieces*
1 pound (450 g) arugula (rocket) leaves, coarsely chopped
1 tablespoon finely grated lemon zest
Kosher salt and freshly ground black pepper to taste
1 tablespoon brandy
3 tablespoons (45 ml) extra-virgin olive oil
2 tablespoons chopped fresh flat-leaf parsley

1. In a medium-sized stockpot, combine the clam juice with 2½ cups (625 ml) of water and bring to a simmer over medium-high heat. Reduce the heat to medium or medium-low to keep the liquid barely simmering.

2. In a large, heavy stockpot, heat the olive oil over medium heat. Add the garlic and cook for 3 to 5 minutes, until golden brown. Using a slotted spoon, remove the garlic from the oil and discard.

3. Raise the heat to medium-high, add the rice, and stir for about 15 seconds, or until the grains are well coated with oil.

4. Add the wine and stir constantly, being careful to scrape the sides and bottom of the pan gently so that the rice does not stick. When the wine is almost gone, add ½ cup (120 ml) of the simmering stock and stir until the stock is nearly absorbed by the rice. Repeat, adding another ½ cup of the stock after each preceding amount has been almost absorbed, until all the stock is used. The entire process will take 17 or 18 minutes. It is very important to stir the rice constantly for even cooking and a creamy texture, although it will remain al dente.

7. When all the broth has been used, add the shrimp, arugula, and lemon zest, stirring gently to mix. Cook for about 3 minutes, or until the flavors blend and the shrimp turn pink and are cooked through. Season with salt and pepper to taste.

8. Remove from the heat and add the brandy. Stir vigorously for 30 seconds to incorporate the brandy. Divide the risotto among 6 plates. Drizzle with the extra-virgin olive oil, garnish with parsley, and serve immediately.

SERVES 6

Vincent learned this classic risotto while working in Venice, and our customers never tire of it. You can use another crustacean (crayfish, lobster, crab) if you like, but shrimp are easy to find and taste wonderful. The addition of clam juice imparts good flavor, but if you want to make a simple stock from the shrimp shells, use it instead for a superb, fresh taste. (Make enough stock for 5 cups and omit the clam juice and water.)

We've been making this version of the Italian classic since the day we opened, and it continues to be a popular dish—even if you are not sure you like calamari (squid), you will like this! Working with the calamari is far easier and more manageable than you might imagine. It's important not to fill the tubes completely, since they shrink during cooking and too much filling can cause them to split or even to explode in the oven. We often serve this dish with Creamy Polenta (page 108) or another mild side dish. One of the best things about it is that it is almost better if made a day in advance and then reheated before serving.

Stuffed Calamari

CALAMARI
½ cup (120 ml) olive oil
1 cup (115 g) chopped onions
14 large tubes calamari (squid) with tentacles
2 teaspoons chopped garlic
1 teaspoon crushed red pepper flakes
½ cup (120 ml) dry white wine
4 large eggs
1 tablespoon chopped fresh basil
1 tablespoon chopped fresh flat-leaf parsley
¾ cup (85 g) fine dry bread crumbs
Salt and freshly ground black pepper

BRAISING LIQUID
3 cups (750 ml) tomato puree
½ cup (120 ml) dry white wine
3 tablespoons (45 ml) olive oil
1 tablespoon chopped fresh basil
2 teaspoons chopped garlic
1 teaspoon crushed red pepper flakes
Salt to taste

1. To prepare the calamari, in a skillet, heat 1 tablespoon of the olive oil and cook the onions gently over medium-low heat for about 30 minutes, until very soft and translucent. (This step can be done ahead of time.)

2. Meanwhile, clean the calamari by separating the tentacles from the tubes. Select 12 of the largest, most intact tubes and refrigerate. Chop the remaining tubes and the tentacles and set aside.

3. In a large sauté pan, heat the remaining oil and cook the garlic over medium-high for 2 to 3 minutes, until golden brown. Remove the pan from the heat and set aside to cool to room temperature. When cool, add the chopped calamari, cooked onions, and red pepper flakes and return the pan to the stove. Heat slowly over very low heat.

4. Gradually bring the mixture to a simmer and add the wine. Cook over medium-low heat for about 45 minutes, until the liquid is reduced by three-quarters.

5. Preheat the oven to 350°F (175°C).

6. In a bowl, beat the eggs with a fork and add the basil and parsley. Pour the egg mixture into the pan and cook, stirring continuously, for about 2 minutes, until the eggs begin to set. Remove the pan from the heat, add the bread crumbs, season to taste with salt and pepper, and set aside to cool.

7. With a small spoon or a pastry bag with no tip, stuff the reserved squid tubes with the mixture, taking care to stuff them only about two-thirds full. Use toothpicks to hold the ends of the tubes closed. You will need approximately 2½ cups of filling; reserve any leftover filling. Arrange the stuffed tubes in a single layer in a baking dish.

8. Make the braising liquid by mixing the tomato puree, wine, olive oil, basil, garlic, and red pepper flakes together and seasoning to taste with salt. Stir the leftover stuffing mixture into the braising liquid. Pour over the calamari, cover the pan with foil, and bake for about 1 hour, or until the calamari are very tender.

SERVES 6

Note: Cooking the calamari on low heat during the early stages of cooking allows it to release its liquid and keeps it tender. It's important not to stuff the tubes too tightly because they shrink by at least a third during baking.

Whole Roasted Chicken with Lemon, Sage, and Bruschetta Stuffing

Eight ¾-inch-thick (2-cm) slices Tuscan Bread (page 173) or other
*   peasant-style bread*
2 large cloves garlic
½ cup (120 ml) extra-virgin olive oil
Kosher salt
Zest of 2 lemons, finely chopped
1 tablespoon chopped fresh sage
Two 3-pound (1.4-kg) chickens, rinsed and patted dry

1. Preheat the oven to 350°F (175°C).

2. To make the bruschetta stuffing, toast or grill the bread until golden brown.

3. Holding a clove of garlic between your thumb and forefinger, rub it over both sides of a slice of bread. Repeat with the remaining slices, using both cloves if necessary.

4. Cut the bread into ½-inch (1.3-cm) cubes (about 4 cups) and put the cubes in a large bowl. Drizzle with 6 tablespoons (90 ml) of the oil and sprinkle with ½ teaspoon salt. Add the lemon zest and sage and mix well.

5. Spoon the bruschetta stuffing into the cavities of the chickens, packing it firmly but not too tightly. Close the cavities, either by sewing them loosely with butcher's twine or by fastening them with toothpicks. If you wish, tie the legs together with twine. Rub each chicken with 1 tablespoon of oil, season with salt, and transfer to a large roasting pan. Roast for about 1½ hours, until the chicken is done and the juices run clear when the leg meat is pierced with a sharp knife and/or a meat thermometer inserted into the thickest part of the thigh meat registers 180° to 185°F (82° to 85°C).

6. To serve, remove the stuffing, then carve and serve the chicken with the stuffing.

SERVES 6

Note: *The bruschetta stuffing can be prepared in advance and refrigerated, covered, for several hours.*

In Italy roasted chicken is often served on top of bruschetta, so when we decided to offer a stuffed chicken, we played with this idea. The wonderful flavors of the lemon and sage come through in this recipe, and as the chicken cooks, the bread is moistened by the cooking juices. This is an excellent way to use day-old Tuscan or peasant-style bread, which does not keep well since it has no preservatives.

Pork roasts are nearly always flavored with rosemary and garlic in Tuscany, and while rosemary is a relatively strong-tasting herb, you want to use a lot of it here. We set the pork roast on a bed of onions, garlic, and rosemary and add a little stock and wine, which makes a wonderful sauce. When this appears on the restaurant menu, we usually make an extra roast so that we can offer pork sandwiches the next day, made with focaccia, a little bit of rosemary, and mayonnaise. Be sure to cook a large enough roast so that you have leftovers too. They're great!

Porchetta Arrosto
ROAST PORK WITH GARLIC AND ROSEMARY

3 tablespoons (45 ml) olive oil
½ cup (55 g) chopped garlic (about 1 head)
3 tablespoons chopped fresh rosemary
Salt and freshly ground black pepper
One 8-pound (3.6-kg) fresh ham, boned and butterflied, bones reserved
    (see Note)
1 pound (450 g) onions, julienned (about 4 cups)
12 whole cloves garlic
3 sprigs fresh rosemary
2 cups (500 ml) dry white wine
2 cups (500 ml) Chicken Stock (page 171)

1. Preheat the oven to 400°F (200°C).

2. In a small bowl, combine the olive oil, chopped garlic, chopped rosemary, about 1½ tablespoons of pepper, and salt to taste. Mix well and then spread the mixture on the inside of the ham. Roll the ham up and tie with kitchen twine in several places to hold securely.

3. In a roasting pan, position the reserved bones to act as a rack for the ham. Surround the bones with the onions, whole garlic cloves, and rosemary sprigs. Set the ham on the bones and pour the wine and stock into the pan. Cover tightly with foil and roast for 2 hours. Remove the foil and insert a meat thermometer into the thickest part of the meat. Roast for about 45 minutes, or until the internal temperature reaches 160°F (72°C) and the meat is very brown.

4. Lift the ham from the pan and set aside on a warm platter. Cover with foil to keep warm and let the ham sit for about 30 minutes.

5. Strain the pan juices through a fine sieve into a saucepan, pressing on the solids to extract as much liquid as possible. Simmer on medium-high heat for about 30 minutes, until reduced to 1½ cups (375 ml). Season to taste with salt and defat the sauce if desired. Slice the ham and serve with the sauce drizzled over the slices.

SERVES 6 TO 8

Note: You may have to order a fresh ham (leg of pork) from the butcher several days before preparing it. Ask the butcher to bone and butterfly it, reserving the bones.

Flourless Rosemary Torta

1 cup (2 sticks/230 g) unsalted butter, softened to room temperature
1 cup (200 g) sugar
1 tablespoon finely chopped fresh rosemary
1 tablespoon finely chopped lemon zest
2 large eggs, separated
1½ teaspoons baking powder
1⅓ cups (185 g) plus 1 tablespoon potato starch (see Note)

1. Preheat the oven to 325°F (165°C). Butter a 10-inch (25-cm) springform pan and dust it with a little potato starch, tapping out the excess.

2. In the bowl of an electric mixer fitted with the paddle attachment and set on medium-high speed, cream the butter and sugar for 3 to 4 minutes, until light and fluffy. Add the rosemary and lemon zest and beat just to incorporate.

3. With the mixer still running, add the egg yolks and baking powder, mixing until incorporated.

4. Reduce the mixing speed to low and add the potato starch, mixing for about 20 seconds. Turn off the mixer and scrape the sides of the bowl. Continue to mix at medium-low speed for about 1 minute longer, until well mixed.

5. In a clean, dry bowl and using clean, dry beaters, whip the egg whites until stiff peaks form. Using a rubber spatula, gently fold the whites into the batter. There will be a few specks of the whites showing. Scrape the batter into the prepared pan; it will fill the pan by only a third to a half and will rise as it bakes. Bake for about 40 minutes, until a toothpick inserted in the center comes out clean. Let the cake cool in the pan on a wire rack for 20 minutes. Carefully run a knife around the edge of the pan and release the sides of the pan. Let the cake cool completely before cutting into wedges to serve.

SERVES 6 TO 8

Note: Potato starch is also called potato starch flour and is sold in health food stores.

This light, tender cake is delicious served on its own or with sweetened whipped cream, sliced fresh fruit or berries, or lemon or orange sorbet. Because it is made without flour, it is best if served on the day it is baked. It does not keep well.

Lemon Buttermilk Pound Cake with Mascarpone Whipped Cream

Vincent has been making this pound cake for years, and it has become a great favorite at the restaurant. He likes to serve it with blueberries because of the sublime combination of blueberries and lemon, but any combination of spring and summer fruit tastes great. The mascarpone whipped cream is the ultimate luxury. While the recipe easily serves 12, make it when serving fewer and enjoy the leftovers.

POUND CAKE

3 cups (525 g) all-purpose (plain) flour
1½ teaspoons baking powder
½ teaspoon ground cinnamon
¼ teaspoon salt
1 cup (2 sticks/230 g) unsalted butter, softened
½ cup (100 g) granulated sugar
½ cup (85 g) lightly packed light or dark brown sugar
3 large eggs
¾ cup (180 ml) buttermilk
2 tablespoons finely chopped lemon zest
2 tablespoons fresh lemon juice

MASCARPONE WHIPPED CREAM

1½ cups (375 ml) heavy (double) cream
½ cup (115 g) mascarpone cheese
½ cup (120 ml) honey

TOPPINGS

3 cups (500 g) blueberries (bilberries), raspberries, or sliced
   strawberries
Confectioners' (icing) sugar, for dusting

1. Preheat the oven to 325°F (165°C). Butter and flour a 2-quart (2-l) Bundt pan, tapping out the excess flour.

2. In a small bowl, whisk together the flour, baking powder, cinnamon, and salt.

3. In the bowl of an electric mixer set on medium speed, beat the butter and sugars for about 5 minutes, until fluffy and light. Scrape the sides of the bowl once or twice during beating. Add the eggs one at a time, beating for about 20 seconds after each addition to incorporate.

(continued on page 40)

4. With the mixer set on low, add the dry ingredients a little at a time, alternating with the buttermilk and ending with the dry ingredients. Scrape the sides of the bowl. Add the lemon zest and lemon juice and mix just until incorporated.

5. Using a rubber spatula, scrape the batter into the prepared pan and tap it several times on the countertop to deflate any air pockets in the batter. Bake on the center rack of the oven for about 1 hour 15 minutes, or until a toothpick inserted in the center comes out clean, the cake begins to pull away from the sides of the pan, and the top is a deep golden brown. Cool completely on a wire rack.

6. Meanwhile, just before serving, make the whipped cream. In the bowl of an electric mixer set on medium-high, combine the cream, mascarpone cheese, and honey and beat until soft peaks form.

7. Turn the cake out onto a serving plate and slice. Spoon the blueberries over or around the cake, top each serving with a dollop of whipped cream, and dust each with confectioners' sugar.

SERVES 12

Note: The cake can be made up to 2 days ahead of time, wrapped well, and refrigerated. Bring to room temperature before serving.

Prosecco-Honey Granita

One 750-milliliter bottle prosecco, dry champagne, or other
  sparkling wine
½ cup (120 ml) fresh lemon juice
1 cup (250 ml) honey

1. In a bowl, combine the prosecco, lemon juice, and honey. Fill the prosecco bottle with water and add to the bowl. Stir until the honey dissolves. Transfer to a shallow stainless steel pan that fits easily in the freezer.

2. Freeze for about 1 hour. Remove and, using a pastry scraper or metal spatula, scrape the sides and bottom of the granita, mixing the frozen particles into the less frozen center.

3. Freeze for about 2 hours longer and scrape again. Let the granita freeze for 3 to 4 hours longer, or until completely frozen. Chop the granita into pieces and serve immediately or return to the freezer until ready to serve.

MAKES ABOUT 2 QUARTS

Note: Prosecco is an Italian sparkling wine, which you may have to order from the liquor store one or two days ahead of time.

This soothing, refreshing granita is a favorite with us. It's especially good with spring or summer berries or sliced fruit.

antipasti

In Italy antipasto is the first course eaten at a meal. It can consist of anything from a plate of sliced meats to a platter with a selection of marinated vegetables and seafood. Antipasto can be as simple, too, as a dish of roasted red peppers or a small bowl of olives. Because their purpose is to stimulate the appetite for the meal to come, antipasto dishes are small. While even a small sampling of dishes is appetizing, in the restaurant we offer a large selection (10 to 12 different antipasti) on the antipasto table and assemble a plate with a little bit of each one. We've gathered some of our favorites on these pages to encompass a spectrum of flavors and textures. Some, such as the Olives Marinated with Cumin and Orange and the Pickled Beets, can be made well in advance. Others are best made 8 to 24 hours ahead of time, while a few need to be prepared shortly before they will be served.

Marinated Roasted Red Peppers

(photograph on page 46)

½ cup (120 ml) extra-virgin olive oil
12 red bell peppers (capsicums)
1 teaspoon finely chopped garlic
Salt to taste
¼ cup (10 g) chiffonade of basil

1. Preheat the oven to 500°F (260°C).

2. Using 2 tablespoons of the oil, rub the peppers with oil and arrange them on a baking sheet. Roast for 10 to 15 minutes, until the skins turn dark and begin to blister. Transfer the peppers to a bowl and cover tightly with plastic wrap (cling film). Set aside for about 10 minutes to steam and cool.

3. When cool enough to handle, rub the skins from the peppers. Cut the peppers in half, scrape out and discard the seeds, and put the peppers in a bowl. Add the remaining olive oil and the garlic and season to taste with salt. Let the peppers marinate at room temperature for at least 20 minutes or longer in the refrigerator. To serve, toss with the basil.

SERVES 6

Olives Marinated with Cumin and Orange

4 cups (450 g) drained whole mixed olives, such as picholine, kalamata, or black or green Spanish or Italian olives
½ cup (120 ml) olive oil

1 tablespoon chopped garlic
1 tablespoon ground cumin
1 teaspoon crushed red pepper flakes
Juice of 1 large navel orange (about ½ cup/120 ml)
Zest of 1 large navel orange, finely chopped

1. Rinse the olives and drain them of excess water in a colander. Transfer to a large glass or ceramic bowl.

2. Add the olive oil, garlic, cumin, red pepper flakes, orange juice, and orange zest and stir to mix. Cover tightly and refrigerate for at least 2 days before serving.

MAKES 1 QUART

Note: These olives will keep in the refrigerator for up to 2 weeks. For spicier olives, increase the amounts of cumin and red pepper flakes.

Eggplant Caponata with Mint

(photograph on page 46)

½ cup (120 ml) plus 2 tablespoons olive oil
3 pounds (1.4 kg) eggplant (aubergines) (about 3 medium), cut into ½-inch (1.3-cm) cubes
Kosher salt to taste
2 to 3 red onions (about 1 pound/450 g), cut into ½-inch (1.3-cm) slices
½ cup (55 g) drained capers
½ cup (120 ml) extra-virgin olive oil
¾ cup (180 ml) red wine vinegar
2 tablespoons sugar
½ teaspoon crushed red pepper flakes
5 tablespoons (14 g) finely chopped fresh mint leaves
1 cup (250 ml) tomato puree
4 teaspoons unsweetened cocoa powder

15 to 16 Sicilian black or green olives, pitted and sliced (about ½ cup/55 g)
½ cup (85 g) raisins

1. Preheat the oven to 400°F (200°C). Rub a large rimmed baking sheet (jelly-roll pan) with about 2 tablespoons of the olive oil.

2. In a large bowl, toss the eggplant with ¼ cup (60 ml) of the olive oil and about 1 teaspoon of salt. Spread the eggplant on the baking sheet and roast for 30 to 40 minutes, until the eggplant is tender and golden brown, tossing carefully once during baking. Let the eggplant cool on the baking sheet. When cool, remove from the sheet and set aside.

3. Using the remaining ¼ cup of olive oil, brush the onion slices. Lay them on the oiled baking sheet (add more oil if necessary) and season with about 1 teaspoon of salt. Roast the onions for about 30 minutes, until tender and golden brown. Let the onions cool on the baking sheet, then cut into ½-inch (1.3-cm) pieces.

4. In a small bowl, combine the capers and enough cold water to cover by about 1 inch and soak for about 20 minutes. Drain.

5. In a large bowl, combine the extra-virgin olive oil, vinegar, sugar, red pepper flakes, mint, tomato puree, and cocoa and stir until the sugar and cocoa are dissolved. Add the eggplant, onions, olives, capers, and raisins and mix well. Cover and refrigerate for at least 24 hours before serving.

MAKES ABOUT 6 CUPS

Note: You may find it easier to use 2 baking sheets when roasting the eggplant. If so, be sure both are well oiled. The caponata will keep in the refrigerator for up to 3 days.

Escarole with Olives, Raisins, and Pine Nuts

(photograph on page 46)

> *¼ cup (30 g) pine nuts (pine kernels) (1 ounce)*
> *½ cup (85 g) raisins*
> *3 pounds (1.4 kg) escarole (chicory) (3 to 4 bunches)*
> *½ cup (120 ml) olive oil*
> *4 teaspoons chopped garlic*
> *Kosher salt to taste*
> *Crushed red pepper flakes to taste*
> *About 20 oil-cured black olives, pitted and halved*
> *   (about ⅓ cup/45 g)*

1. Preheat the oven to 350°F (175°C).

2. Spread the pine nuts in a single layer on a baking sheet and toast for 4 to 5 minutes, until fragrant and golden brown. Shake the pan once or twice during toasting and take care that the nuts do not burn. Transfer to a plate to cool.

3. In a bowl, combine the raisins with enough warm water to cover by about 1 inch (2.5 cm) and set aside to plump for about 20 minutes. Drain.

4. Trim the root end from the escarole and discard any tough or bruised outer leaves. Rinse the leaves to remove any sand. Bring a large pot of water to a boil and blanch the escarole for 4 to 5 minutes, until wilted. Drain well and spread out on a work surface or baking sheet to cool. You may have to do this in 2 batches.

5. In a Dutch oven or large pot, heat the oil on medium heat and sauté the garlic for about 1 minute, until golden brown. Add the escarole and season with about 1½ teaspoons of the salt and red pepper flakes to taste. Raise the heat to high and cook for about 5 minutes, stirring constantly. Add the raisins and olives, reduce the heat to medium-high, and cook, stirring and tossing, for 6 to 8 minutes, until any moisture from the escarole evaporates.

6. Transfer the escarole mixture to a platter and sprinkle with the pine nuts. Serve warm or at room temperature.

MAKES ABOUT 4 CUPS

Note: Vincent prefers this served at room temperature.

Insalata Rossa

(photograph on page 46)

This is a fresh-tasting summer salad that can be served as antipasto or as a side dish with grilled chicken, steak, or shrimp. It is also good spooned over salad greens. The red color comes from the beets (beetroot), which makes it especially pretty.

> *1 cup (150 g) trimmed green beans, cut into*
> *   ½-inch lengths (about ⅓ pound)*
> *1 cup (150 g) peeled, finely diced potatoes*
> *   (about ⅓ pound)*
> *1 cup (225 g) peeled, finely diced Pickled Beets*
> *   (recipe follows)*
> *1 cup (115 g) finely diced red onions*
> *1 cup (230 g) seeded, finely diced tomatoes*
> *½ cup (120 ml) olive oil*
> *½ cup (120 ml) balsamic vinegar*
> *¼ cup (10 g) thinly sliced fresh basil leaves*
> *Kosher salt and freshly ground black pepper*
> *   to taste*

1. Bring a pot of water to a boil over high heat, add the green beans, and cook for 2 minutes. Set a bowl of cold

water next to the sink. Drain the beans and plunge them into the cold water, so that they retain their bright green color.

2. Put the potatoes in the same pot and add enough cold water to cover them by about an inch. Bring to a boil, reduce the heat, and cook for 4 to 5 minutes, until the potatoes are fork tender. Drain and rinse under cold water.

3. Put the beets in a bowl. Drain the beans and add them and the potatoes to the beets. Add the onions, tomatoes, oil, vinegar, and basil. Season with salt and pepper.

4. Cover and refrigerate for at least 8 hours or overnight to marinate.

SERVES 6

Pickled Beets

*2 pounds (900 g) beets (beetroot), trimmed but
    not peeled, scrubbed under running water*
2 cups (500 ml) distilled white vinegar
¾ cup (150 g) sugar
½ cup (120 ml) honey
2 tablespoons salt
1 teaspoon whole black peppercorns
One 3-inch (7.5-cm) cinnamon stick

1. In a large pot, combine all the ingredients and add about 2 quarts (2 l) of water. The beets should be covered by at least 1 inch (2.5 cm) of liquid. Add more water if necessary.

2. Bring to a boil over high heat. Reduce the heat and simmer, uncovered, for about 45 minutes, until the beets are fork tender (not soft). Remove from the heat and let the beets cool in the cooking liquid.

3. Use immediately or transfer the beets and the cooking liquid to a container with a lid and refrigerate until ready to use. The beets will keep in the refrigerator for up to 1 month.

MAKES ABOUT 2 POUNDS (900 G)

Beet Salad with Goat Cheese and Walnuts

*1 recipe Pickled Beets (recipe precedes), cooled
    and cut into ½-inch (1.3-cm) cubes*
½ cup (55 g) toasted chopped walnuts
¼ cup (30 g) finely chopped red onion
½ cup (120 ml) extra-virgin olive oil
¼ cup (60 ml) balsamic vinegar
1 teaspoon coarsely ground black pepper
½ teaspoon kosher salt
¾ cup (115 g) crumbled goat cheese (chèvre)
1 tablespoon finely chopped fresh flat-leaf parsley

1. In a glass or ceramic bowl, combine the beets, walnuts, and onion and stir gently to mix.

2. In another bowl, whisk together the olive oil, vinegar, pepper, and salt. Add to the beets and walnuts and stir gently. Cover and set aside to marinate for 30 minutes at room temperature.

3. Transfer the beets to a serving plate and sprinkle with goat cheese and parsley.

MAKES ABOUT 5 CUPS

Cannellini with Tuna

When we traveled in Portofino, a dish similar to this was on half the lunch menus, and although at the restaurant we serve it as antipasto, it makes a great light lunch dish. It's important to use tuna that is packed in olive oil, which may be hard to find. Tuna packed in vegetable oil or water won't have the same good flavor. It is equally important not to use white (albacore) tuna, which is too mild tasting. At the restaurant we make this with fresh tuna, which we roast and then marinate overnight in olive oil.

> 1 pound dried cannellini (white kidney beans), picked over and rinsed
> 6 large cloves garlic
> One 6-inch (15-cm) sprig fresh rosemary
> One 6-inch (15-cm) leafy sprig fresh sage
> 1 cup (115 g) diced red onions
> ¼ cup (10 g) chopped fresh flat-leaf parsley
> 1 cup (250 ml) olive oil
> ¾ cup (180 ml) red wine vinegar
> 2 cans (12 ounces/340 g) Italian or Spanish chunk tuna packed in olive oil
> Salt and freshly ground black pepper to taste

1. To prepare the beans, place them in a large pot, cover with cold water, and soak for 6 to 8 hours or overnight. Drain, discarding the soaking water, rinse, and drain again.

2. In a large pot, combine the beans, garlic, rosemary, and sage and add enough cold water to cover by 4 inches (10 cm). Bring to a boil over high heat, reduce the heat, and simmer for about 1 hour, or until the beans are just tender. Drain the beans, reserving the cooking liquid. Transfer the cooking liquid to a metal bowl set over a larger bowl filled with ice cubes. When the beans have cooled slightly, add them to the chilled cooking liquid. Cover and refrigerate unless using right away.

3. Transfer the beans to a large bowl. Remove the leaves from the rosemary and sage sprigs and add them to the beans. Add the onions, parsley, oil, and vinegar and toss lightly.

4. Add the tuna and toss it with the beans, taking care to break it into bite-sized chunks but no smaller. Season to taste with salt and pepper, then cover and refrigerate for at least 2 hours to marinate. Serve chilled.

SERVES 6

Note: This can be made 1 or 2 days in advance and refrigerated, covered. To quick-soak the beans, place them in a large pot, cover with water, bring to a boil over high heat, and cook for about 2 minutes. Remove from the heat and let stand for 1 hour. Drain and discard the liquid and proceed with step 3 of the recipe.

Clockwise from left: Cannellini with Tuna; Escarole with Olives, Raisins, and Pine Nuts (recipe on page 44); Insalata Rossa (recipe on page 44); Eggplant Caponata with Mint (recipe on page 43); Marinated Roasted Red Peppers (recipe on page 42)

SUMMER

Many of our summertime recipes include corn (maize) because, as Americans, we treasure the sweet corn available to us during the summer season. For this recipe, we have added chopped tomatoes and basil in an effort to "Italianize" the soup (Italians do not make corn chowder). We don't use a stock base but instead make corn stock by boiling the corn cobs in water. This produces a surprisingly delicious and easy base for the soup. At first glance, the soup looks thick and creamy, but actually it is quite light.

Page 49: Pappardelle with Summer Corn and Fresh Tomatoes (recipe on page 57)

Corn Chowder

6 ears fresh corn, shucked
3 yellow (brown) onions, coarsely chopped
1 teaspoon salt, plus more to taste
¾ pound (340 g) thick-cut or slab bacon, diced (about 2 cups)
3 large potatoes, peeled and diced
2 cups (500 ml) heavy (double) cream
½ cup (20 g) loosely packed torn basil leaves
Freshly ground black pepper
About 1 cup (230 g) seeded, chopped tomatoes

1. In a large pot of boiling water over high heat, blanch the corn for about 3 minutes. Transfer to a bowl of cold water to stop the cooking. Using a sharp knife, cut the kernels from the cobs and set the kernels aside. You will have about 3½ cups (400 g).

2. Chop the cobs into 1-inch (2.5-cm) chunks or break each one into 2 to 3 pieces. Transfer the cobs and 1 of the chopped onions to a large pot and add 4½ quarts (4.5 l) of water. Stir in 1 teaspoon of salt and bring the water to a boil over high heat. Reduce the heat to medium-high and cook, uncovered, for 50 to 60 minutes, until reduced by half (about 9 cups). Strain the liquid into a large saucepan and discard the solids.

3. In a large pot over medium-low heat, slowly cook the bacon for about 30 minutes, until it is crisp and the fat is rendered. Discard half the fat. Add the remaining onions to the pot and cook for 3 to 4 minutes, until the onions begin to soften. Add the corn stock, reserved corn kernels, and potatoes. Bring to a boil over high heat. Reduce the heat to medium and cook, uncovered, for about 15 minutes, until the potatoes soften. Add the cream and basil and cook for about 5 minutes longer, until heated through and the flavors blend. Season to taste with salt and pepper. Serve garnished with chopped tomatoes.

SERVES 6 TO 8

Chicken Soup with Escarole and Orzo

¼ cup (60 ml) olive oil
2 cups (230 g) julienned onions
3 tablespoons chopped garlic
5 cups (450 g) chopped escarole (chicory) (about 1 pound)
1 to 2 teaspoons crushed red pepper flakes, or to taste
3 quarts (3 l) Chicken Stock (page 171)
½ pound (230 g) roasted chicken meat, cut into small pieces (about
   2 cups)
1 cup (140 g) orzo
Kosher salt to taste
1 cup (115 g) freshly grated Parmesan cheese

1. In a large, heavy stockpot, heat the oil over medium heat. Add the onions and garlic and cook, covered, for about 15 minutes, until the onions are translucent.

2. Add the escarole and red pepper flakes and cook for about 2 minutes, until the escarole wilts.

3. Add the stock and bring to a boil over high heat. Reduce the heat to medium-high and simmer for 20 minutes.

4. Add the chicken and orzo and cook for 5 to 6 minutes, until the orzo is tender. Season to taste with salt. Ladle the soup into serving bowls and garnish with cheese.

SERVES 6

Note: Use leftover roasted chicken or roast a 1-pound (450-g) breast with the bone in. The breast will yield about ½ pound (230 g) of meat when pulled off the bone. The soup can be made a day in advance without the chicken and orzo. Add them just before serving, cooking as directed in step 4.

A variation on an Italian-American recipe often called "wedding soup," this version can be served summer or winter (for instance, we serve it on Valentine's Day). Marion remembers that when she was young, a similar soup was served at every wedding she attended—a continuation of a tradition followed in Italy, where the soup is always followed by a pasta course and then a meat course. The original recipe contains meatballs, but we lightened it by substituting pieces of chicken.

Pappa al Pomodoro

1 pound (450 g) leeks
1 cup (250 ml) olive oil
3 tablespoons chopped garlic
2 teaspoons crushed red pepper flakes, or to taste
2 pounds (900 g) tomatoes, peeled, seeded, and chopped, or two 28-ounce (800-g) cans tomatoes, drained and chopped
6 cups (1.5 l) Chicken Stock (page 171)
½ cup (20 g) loosely packed torn fresh basil leaves
2 tablespoons honey
4 cups (about 115 g) loosely packed Tuscan Bread cubes (see Note)
½ cup (55 g) freshly grated Parmesan cheese

1. Prepare the leeks by trimming off the green stems and slicing the white parts in half lengthwise, then cutting crosswise to make ½-inch-wide (1.3-cm) half-moon shapes. Transfer to a bowl of cold water and let stand for about 5 minutes. During this time, any sand in the leeks will sink to the bottom of the bowl. Scoop the leeks from the bowl and drain.

2. In a large pot, heat the oil over medium-low heat and add the leeks, garlic, and red pepper flakes. Cook, uncovered, stirring often, for 20 to 25 minutes, until the leeks soften.

3. Add the tomatoes, stock, basil, and honey, raise the heat to medium-high, and bring to a boil, stirring to break up the tomatoes. Reduce the heat to medium and simmer, uncovered, for about 30 minutes, until the flavors blend. Add the bread and cheese and simmer gently over medium-low heat for about 30 minutes, until the bread is incorporated into the soup. Season with salt and serve immediately.

SERVES 6

Note: Use Tuscan Bread (page 173) or another peasant-style bread. Four cups is about 4 ounces (115 g) of bread, or half a regular-sized loaf.

Roasted Potato Salad

2 pounds (900 g) small Red Bliss (thin-skinned) potatoes, quartered but
  not peeled
3 tablespoons (45 ml) olive oil
Kosher salt and freshly ground black pepper to taste
½ cup (115 g) julienned Roasted Red Peppers (page 168)
½ cup (55 g) diced red onions
¼ cup (10 g) chopped fresh flat-leaf parsley
¼ cup (10 g) chopped fresh basil
¼ cup (55 g) mayonnaise
¼ cup (60 ml) buttermilk

1. Preheat the oven to 400°F (200°C).

2. In a bowl, toss the potatoes with the olive oil and season to taste with salt and pepper.

3. Spread the potatoes in a single layer on a baking sheet and roast for 50 to 60 minutes, until browned and tender. Toss the potatoes several times during roasting.

4. Transfer the potatoes to a bowl and let them cool just until warm. Add the roasted peppers, onions, parsley, basil, mayonnaise, and buttermilk and toss. Season to taste with salt and pepper if necessary, and serve warm or at room temperature.

SERVES 6; MAKES ABOUT 2 QUARTS

Note: If refrigerated, let the salad return to room temperature before serving.

Roasting the potatoes for this otherwise fairly traditional potato salad gives it a texture different from that of a salad made with boiled potatoes. We serve this all summer long with any number of entrees.

Marion Scotto's Poached Artichokes with Tomato and Onion Salad

ARTICHOKES

4 lemons

6 large artichokes

2 cups (500 ml) dry white wine

8 whole cloves garlic

3 tablespoons salt

1 tablespoon black peppercorns

6 sprigs fresh thyme

3 sprigs fresh rosemary

TOMATO SALAD

2 large tomatoes, peeled, seeded, and cut into ¼-inch dice

½ cup (55 g) finely chopped red onion

3 tablespoons chopped fresh basil

¼ cup (60 ml) extra-virgin olive oil, plus more for drizzling

¼ cup (60 ml) balsamic vinegar

Kosher salt and freshly ground black pepper to taste

1. In a large bowl or pot, combine 2 quarts (2 l) of water and the juice of 2 of the lemons to make acidulated water. Drop the squeezed lemons in the water.

2. Prepare the artichokes by snipping off the thorny ends of the leaves. Using your fingers, push the leaves apart to expose the choke. Use a teaspoon or serrated grapefruit spoon to scoop out and discard the choke, taking care to remove the whole choke. As each artichoke is finished, drop it in the lemon water.

3. In a large stockpot, combine the wine, garlic, salt, peppercorns, thyme, rosemary, and juice of the remaining 2 lemons with approximately 3 quarts (3 l) of water to make a court bouillon. Bring to a boil over high heat and add the artichokes. When all are in the pot, invert a heatproof dinner plate on top of the artichokes to keep them submerged. Return the court bouillon to a boil, reduce the heat to medium, and simmer for about 50 minutes, until the artichokes are fork-tender.

4. Remove the pot from the heat and set aside for 30 minutes to allow the artichokes to cool slightly. Lift the artichokes from the court bouillon and cool them completely in the refrigerator. Discard the court bouillon.

5. To make the salad, combine the tomatoes and onion in a bowl and toss gently. Add the basil, olive oil, vinegar, and salt and pepper to taste and toss to mix.

6. Trim the bottoms of the artichokes so that they stand upright. Spoon the salad into the center of the artichokes and drizzle each with a little olive oil.

SERVES 6; MAKES ABOUT 2½ CUPS TOMATO SALAD

Corn, Tomato, and Red Onion Salad

1¾ cups (200 g) fresh corn kernels (from 3 ears)
1¾ cups (400 g) seeded and diced tomatoes
1 small red onion, julienned (about ½ cup/55 g)
¼ cup (10 g) fresh basil chiffonade
½ cup (120 ml) extra-virgin olive oil
¼ cup (60 ml) balsamic vinegar
Salt and freshly ground black pepper to taste
6 sprigs fresh basil, for garnish

1. In a saucepan of boiling water, blanch the corn for 3 minutes. Drain and cool slightly.

2. In a mixing bowl, combine the corn with the tomatoes, onion, basil, olive oil, and vinegar. Toss gently and season to taste with salt and pepper.

3. Transfer to a serving platter and garnish with fresh basil sprigs.

SERVES 6; MAKES ABOUT 1 QUART

When you have beautiful tomatoes and farm-fresh sweet corn (maize), make this salad. With its wonderful combination of flavors, it can serve as a simple first course or a side dish for grilled chicken, steak, or hamburgers. Or spoon it over grilled Italian-style peasant bread for bruschetta. It's important to assemble the salad just before serving. You can cut the corn from the ears and dice the tomatoes ahead of time, but add the oil and vinegar at the last minute.

Bruschetta is a simple open-faced Italian sandwich that has become exceptionally popular in the United States. When tomatoes are at their peak, serve it as part of an antipasto, by itself with cocktails, or as a first course. Tomato salad is a traditional topping for bruschetta, but you can top the bread with nearly any fresh vegetable or seafood combination.

(photograph on page 70)

Anthony Scotto, Jr.'s Bruschetta with Tomatoes

TOMATO SALAD

3 vine-ripened beefsteak tomatoes, cored, seeded, and chopped
½ cup (55 g) julienned red onion
8 fresh basil leaves, coarsely chopped or torn
¼ cup (60 ml) extra-virgin olive oil
3 tablespoons (45 ml) balsamic vinegar
¼ teaspoon freshly ground black pepper
Kosher salt to taste

BRUSCHETTA

6 slices Tuscan Bread (page 173) or other peasant-style bread
¼ cup (60 ml) extra-virgin olive oil
6 whole cloves garlic
Kosher salt to taste

1. To make the salad, in a glass or ceramic bowl, combine the tomatoes, onion, basil, oil, vinegar, and pepper. Stir gently and season to taste with salt. Set aside.

2. Preheat the broiler or preheat the oven to 450°F (230°C).

3. To prepare the bruschetta, lay the bread in a single layer on a baking sheet. Using about half the olive oil, brush each slice with oil. Broil or bake for a few minutes until golden brown.

4. Holding each slice of bread between your thumb and forefinger, rub a garlic clove over the toasted side. Drizzle the bread with more olive oil and sprinkle with salt. Top each slice with the tomato salad and serve immediately.

SERVES 6

Pappardelle with Summer Corn and Fresh Tomatoes

½ pound (230 g) dried pappardelle or other wide noodles (see Note)
½ cup (120 ml) olive oil
2 teaspoons chopped garlic
1 teaspoon crushed red pepper flakes
2½ cups (280 g) fresh corn kernels (from 4 to 5 ears)
6 plum (egg) tomatoes, seeded and diced small (1 pound/450 g;
    about 2½ cups)
¼ cup (10 g) loosely packed fresh sage leaves
Salt to taste
Freshly grated Parmesan cheese, for garnish

1. Bring a large pot of lightly salted water to a boil and cook the pasta for 6 to 8 minutes, until barely al dente. Drain, reserving ½ cup (120 ml) of the cooking water.

2. In a large sauté pan, heat the olive oil over medium heat. Add the garlic and red pepper flakes and sauté for less than 1 minute, until the garlic is soft but not browned.

3. Add the pasta and ¼ cup (60 ml) of the pasta cooking water to the pan and cook over medium-high heat for 3 to 5 minutes, until the water has almost evaporated.

4. Add the corn, tomatoes, and sage. Toss just until warmed and thoroughly mixed. Add salt to taste.

5. Transfer to a serving platter and garnish with Parmesan cheese. Serve immediately.

SERVES 6

Note: *Pappardelle is 1 inch (2.5 cm) wide, making it the widest pasta noodle. It is available in some supermarkets, in Italian groceries, and in specialty stores.*

This recipe exemplifies the kind of cooking we call new Tuscan because it uses only what is fresh and available. There is very little corn (maize) in Italy and certainly not the tender sweet corn we can get in this country, but we are convinced that if Tuscan cooks were exposed to American sweet corn, they would embrace it. This dish pairs two summertime favorites: corn and garden-fresh tomatoes. We also use sage, which goes well with these ingredients, but you can substitute basil or cilantro if you prefer.

(photograph on page 49)

Vincent got this idea from his friend Faith Willinger, who has lived in Florence for the past 20 years. Substituting arugula (rocket) for basil is a delicious variation on the pesto theme. At Fresco we serve the pasta warm, but it is equally good at room temperature.

Arugula Pesto with Pennette

¼ cup (30 g) pine nuts (pine kernels) (about 1 ounce)
1 cup (250 ml) extra-virgin olive oil
6 whole cloves garlic
3 cups (115 g) loosely packed arugula (rocket) leaves
¼ cup (30 g) freshly grated Parmesan cheese
Kosher salt to taste
1½ pounds (675 g) dried pennette or other small pasta such as shells or
    farfalle (small bowties) (see Note)
1 cup (115 g) corn kernels, blanched
1 cup (230 g) peeled, seeded, and chopped tomatoes
4 ounces (115 g) Parmesan cheese

1. Preheat the oven to 350°F (175°C).

2. Spread the pine nuts in a single layer on a baking sheet and toast for 4 to 5 minutes, until fragrant and golden brown. Shake the pan once or twice during toasting and take care that the nuts do not burn. Transfer to a plate to cool.

3. In a blender, combine the olive oil and garlic and process until smooth. Add a quarter of the arugula and process until smooth. Add the rest of the arugula and the pine nuts and process until smooth. Add the cheese and process until smooth. Season to taste with salt if needed.

4. In a large pot of lightly salted boiling water, cook the pasta for 6 to 8 minutes, until al dente. Drain, reserving 1 cup of the pasta cooking water.

5. In a large skillet, combine the pesto and pasta and cook over high heat for about 2 minutes, until heated through. Add some of the reserved pasta water if the sauce seems dry. Remove from the heat and toss with the corn and tomatoes.

6. Divide the pasta among 6 plates. Using a vegetable peeler, peel shavings of cheese onto the top of each.

SERVES 6

Note: Pennette pasta is small penne, about ½ inch (1.3 cm) long, and is available at some Italian markets or specialty stores.

Elaina Scotto's Rigatoni with Sausage and Broccoli Rabe

A popular combination of ingredients comes together in this fast and easy summer pasta, which is equally good at other times of year.

2 pounds (900 g) hot or mild Italian sausage, casings removed and crumbled
¾ pound (340 g) broccoli rabe
¾ cup (180 ml) olive oil
2 tablespoons chopped garlic
1 tablespoon crushed red pepper flakes
¼ cup (10 g) chopped fresh flat-leaf parsley
1 pound (450 g) dried rigatoni pasta
Kosher salt to taste
Freshly grated Parmesan cheese

1. In a large nonstick skillet, cook the sausage over medium-high heat for 3 to 4 minutes, stirring, until browned. Drain and set aside.

2. In a large pot of boiling water, cook the broccoli rabe for about 5 minutes, until fork-tender. Rinse under cold running water and drain. When cool, squeeze out any excess water and coarsely chop. Set aside.

3. In a large sauté pan, heat the olive oil over medium heat and cook the garlic for 30 seconds to 1 minute, until golden brown. Add the red pepper flakes, parsley, broccoli rabe, and sausage. Stir just until heated through.

4. In a large pot of lightly salted boiling water, cook the rigatoni for 8 to 10 minutes, until al dente. Drain and toss well with the broccoli rabe and sausage mixture. Season with salt and serve sprinkled with cheese.

SERVES 6

Note: The sausage and broccoli rabe may be cooked separately up to a day in advance.

Spaghettini with Manila Clams, Olive Oil, Garlic, and Oven-Roasted Tomatoes

1½ pounds (675 g) dried spaghettini
¾ cup (180 ml) olive oil
¾ cup (180 ml) dry white wine
1½ teaspoons chopped garlic
¾ teaspoon crushed red pepper flakes
3 tablespoons chopped flat-leaf parsley, plus more for garnish
3 pounds (1.4 kg) manila, littleneck, or cherrystone clams, well scrubbed (see Note)
18 pieces Oven-Roasted Tomatoes (page 169) or dry-packed sun-dried tomato halves, roughly chopped
Salt to taste

1. Bring a large pot of lightly salted water to a boil and cook the pasta for 6 to 8 minutes, until barely al dente. Drain, reserving ½ cup (120 ml) of the cooking water.

2. In a large sauté pan, heat the olive oil over medium-high heat. Add the wine, garlic, red pepper flakes, parsley, and clams. Cover and cook for 3 to 4 minutes, until the clams open. Discard any that do not open.

3. Add the pasta, tomatoes, and reserved cooking water and cook for 3 to 4 minutes, until the water has almost evaporated. Season to taste with salt. Transfer to a serving platter and garnish with parsley.

SERVES 6

Note: Manila clams are small, sweet clams. You may have to order them from a fishmonger, since they may be hard to find outside major metropolitan areas. Even in a city, it is a good idea to call first to see if the clams are available. If you cannot find them, substitute cherrystone or littleneck clams or cockles, which are becoming increasingly available.

Although this is a traditional dish in southern Italy, we make it every Christmas Eve at Fresco. We have included it with the summer recipes because it's so refreshing in the warm weather, made with fresh seafood marinated in lemon juice, garlic, olive oil, and parsley. This salad is better if made a day ahead of time. It can be served on its own, on bruschetta, or as an antipasto. You can use any seafood you like, but in Italy the salad always includes both octopus and calamari (squid).

Marinated Seafood Salad with Lemon Vinaigrette

SALAD
3 cups (750 ml) white wine
4½ tablespoons black peppercorns
9 cloves garlic
1 carrot, peeled and cut into thick slices
3 tablespoons sugar
6 bay leaves
3 lemons
One 2-pound (900-g) octopus (see Note)
1 pound (450 g) calamari (squid), cut into rings (see Note)
1 pound (450 g) medium shrimp, shelled and deveined
1½ cups (170 g) diced celery

VINAIGRETTE
1 cup (250 ml) extra-virgin olive oil
½ cup (120 ml) fresh lemon juice
3 large cloves garlic, thinly sliced
¼ cup (10 g) chopped fresh flat-leaf parsley
½ teaspoon crushed red pepper flakes, or to taste
Kosher salt to taste
1 cup (115 g) sliced black olives, such as kalamata, for garnish

1. To prepare the salad, in a large stockpot, combine 3 quarts (3 l) water, 1 cup (250 ml) of the wine, 1½ tablespoons of the peppercorns, 3 cloves of the garlic, the carrot, the sugar, and 2 of the bay leaves. Cut 1 of the lemons in half, squeeze the juice of both halves into the water, and drop the lemon in too. Bring to a boil over high heat and then reduce the heat to medium so that the court bouillon simmers. Add the octopus and simmer for about 45 minutes, until tender. Remove the pot from the heat and let the octopus cool in the liquid. Drain and clean by removing the soft purple skin and the suckers. (Do not worry if you don't get all the skin and suckers—they taste good.) Cut the octopus into ½-inch (1.3-cm) pieces.

2. In the same or another pot, combine 3 quarts (3 l) water with the remain-

ing wine, peppercorns, garlic, bay leaves, and lemons. Bring to a boil over high heat and then reduce the heat to medium so that the court bouillon simmers. Add the calamari and cook for about 2 minutes, until tender. Take care not to overcook. Using a slotted spoon, lift the calamari from the pot and spread in a single layer on a flat plate to cool.

3. Let the court bouillon return to a simmer and add the shrimp. Cook for 2 to 3 minutes, until pink and opaque. Drain and cool.

4. In a bowl, combine the octopus, calamari, and shrimp. Add the celery and toss.

5. To make the vinaigrette, in a small bowl, whisk together the oil and lemon juice. Add the garlic, parsley, and red pepper flakes and season to taste with salt. Whisk well and add to the seafood. Cover and refrigerate for at least 12 hours.

6. Just before serving, stir the olives into the salad.

SERVES 6; MAKES ABOUT 2 QUARTS

Note: *As the octopus cooks, it will shrink by about half. You can buy octopus and calamari ready to cook from the fishmonger. Octopus and calamari are also sold frozen in many supermarkets. You can substitute scallops for the octopus or calamari.*

Clams Sautéed with Lemon and Fennel

½ cup (120 ml) extra-virgin olive oil
2 teaspoons chopped garlic
½ cup (120 ml) dry white wine
½ to 1 teaspoon crushed red pepper flakes, or to taste
1 tablespoon ground fennel seed
1 tablespoon grated lemon zest
2 tablespoons fresh lemon juice
3 pounds (1.4 kg) manila, littleneck, or cherrystone clams, well scrubbed
   (see Note)
¾ pound (340 g) plum (egg) tomatoes, cored, seeded, and coarsely
   chopped
¼ cup (10 g) chopped fresh flat-leaf parsley

Nearly every Italian restaurant in New York and elsewhere offers a clam sauce for pasta. While this dish is not served over pasta, it is a variation on the theme with added lemon and fennel, two flavors that combine especially well with clams. For a nice light meal, serve the clams with crusty bread.

(continued on page 64)

1. In a large skillet or stockpot, heat the oil over medium heat. Add the garlic and cook, stirring, for 1 to 2 minutes, until softened and golden brown. Be careful not to burn the garlic.

2. Add the wine, red pepper flakes, fennel seed, lemon zest, and juice. Increase the heat to high and add the clams. Cover and cook for 6 to 8 minutes, until the clams open. Discard any that do not open. Using a slotted spoon, transfer the clams to shallow soup bowls.

3. Add the tomatoes and parsley to the broth, bring to a simmer over medium heat, and cook for 1 minute, just to heat through. Ladle the broth over the clams and serve.

SERVES 6

Note: Manila clams are small, sweet clams. You may have to order them from a fishmonger, since they may be hard to find outside major metropolitan areas. Even in a city, it is a good idea to call first to see if the clams are available. If not, use the smallest fresh clams available. In place of ground fennel seed, crush fennel seeds using a mortar and pestle.

Venetian Seafood Stew

¾ pound (340 g) small red potatoes, halved or quartered but not peeled
1 leek
6 tablespoons (90 ml) olive oil
1 teaspoon chopped garlic
½ teaspoon crushed red pepper flakes
¾ cup (180 ml) Fish Stock (page 170) or bottled clam juice
½ cup (120 ml) dry white wine
1 cup (250 ml) tomato puree
2 pinches saffron threads
24 small mussels, scrubbed and debearded
*1½ pounds (675 g) manila, cherrystone, or littleneck clams, well
    scrubbed (see Note)*
1½ pounds (675 g) monkfish, cut into bite-sized pieces (see Note)

12 large shrimp, peeled and deveined (see Note)
¼ cup (10 g) chopped fresh flat-leaf parsley
Kosher salt to taste

1. Put the potatoes in a saucepan and add enough cold water to cover them by 3 inches. Bring to a boil over high heat and cook, uncovered, for 15 to 20 minutes, until fork-tender. Drain the potatoes and set aside.

2. Meanwhile, prepare the leek by trimming off the green stem and slicing the white part in half lengthwise, then cutting crosswise to make ¼-inch-wide (6-mm) half-moon shapes. Transfer to a bowl of cold water and let stand for about 5 minutes. During this time, any sand in the leek will sink to the bottom of the bowl. Scoop the leek from the bowl and drain.

3. In a large saucepan or Dutch oven, heat the oil over medium-low heat. Add the leek, garlic, and red pepper flakes and cook, stirring, for 12 to 15 minutes, until the leek is very tender but not browned.

4. Add the stock, wine, and tomato puree and bring to a simmer over medium-high heat. Stir in the saffron. Add the mussels, clams, fish, and shrimp and cook for about 5 minutes, until the shellfish open, the monkfish is opaque and cooked through, and the shrimp are pink. Discard any mussels or clams that do not open. Using a slotted spoon, remove the seafood from the pan and transfer to 6 shallow bowls. Put the potatoes and parsley in the pan and bring to a boil over high heat. Cook for about 2 minutes, until heated through, and season to taste with salt. Divide the broth and potatoes among the bowls and serve.

SERVES 6

Note: *Manila clams are small, sweet clams. You may have to order them from a fishmonger, since they can be hard to find outside major metropolitan areas. If you cannot find monkfish, substitute lobster meat (about 1½ pounds/675 g of lobster tails in the shell is enough for this recipe). At the restaurant the chef uses large shrimp with the heads still attached, but these are hard to find in retail markets.*

If you do not have a pan large enough to hold the seafood in a single layer, for even cooking, put the larger pieces in the bottom of the pan and the smaller, faster-cooking pieces (shrimp and monkfish) on top.

The secret to this stew is to use the freshest local seafood available and then to take care not to overcook it. Many stews cook for hours, so that in the final dish everything tastes somewhat alike. In this stew, which only cooks for minutes, you can taste the individual clams, mussels, shrimp, and whatever other seafood is included. Stews like this are common fare in Venice and its environs, and like so many similar dishes, no two are exactly alike, yet none is too different from the other.

Whole Grilled Fish with Summer Herbs

Six 1¼-pound (565-g) whole fish, such as red snapper, bass, trout, or pompano (see Note)
½ cup (20 g) chopped fresh mixed herbs, such as parsley, oregano, thyme, and rosemary
Kosher salt and freshly ground black pepper to taste
About ½ cup (120 ml) olive oil
Extra-virgin olive oil for drizzling

1. Prepare a charcoal or gas grill. Remove the grilling rack and clean it very well. Let the coals get very hot.

2. Lay the fish on a work surface and open them up. Sprinkle the inside of each fish with the herbs and season with salt and pepper. Drizzle each cavity with a little oil. Close the fish and brush them on both sides with more olive oil and season with salt and pepper.

3. Rub the remaining olive oil over the grilling rack. Set the rack 4 to 5 inches (10 to 13 cm) over the fire, and when the oil begins to smoke, lay the fish on the rack.

4. Grill the fish for about 3 minutes. Using 2 large forks slipped between the slats of the rack and the fish, gently lift and rotate each one about 45 degrees and continue grilling for 3 minutes longer. Using the same technique, roll the fish over and grill for 3 minutes. Rotate them again and grill about 3 minutes longer, until the flesh flakes and is opaque. Lift the fish from the grill and serve drizzled with a little extra-virgin olive oil. Remove the heads and tails before serving if desired.

SERVES 6

Note: *Buy the freshest fish available. Freshness is more desirable than a particular kind of fish. When buying whole fish, look for clear eyes and firm flesh that bounces back when pressed with your finger. The fish should not smell of anything but the ocean or fresh water—it should not have a "fishy" odor. The gills should be bright red, never slimy. Once you check the gills, ask the fishmonger to remove them.*

Pan-Seared Scallops with Prosecco

2½ pounds (1.13 g) large sea scallops, halved if necessary
Salt and freshly ground black pepper to taste
4 to 6 tablespoons (60 to 90 ml) olive oil
2 teaspoons chopped fresh garlic
1½ cups (375 ml) prosecco or dry champagne
½ cup (55 g) finely ground toasted, unseasoned bread crumbs
¼ cup (10 g) chopped fresh flat-leaf parsley
2 tablespoons extra-virgin olive oil

1. Spread the scallops on a towel and pat dry. Season with salt and pepper.

2. In a large, heavy skillet, heat 4 tablespoons (60 ml) of the olive oil over medium-high heat until very hot and smoking slightly. Add one-quarter to one-third of the scallops to the skillet to form a single layer without crowding the pan. Sear for 1½ to 2 minutes on each side, until golden brown. Transfer to a plate and set aside. Continue searing the scallops in the same manner in several batches, adding more oil as necessary and making sure the pan regains its high temperature between batches. When all the scallops are on the plate, cover to keep warm and set aside.

3. Reduce the heat to medium, add the garlic, and sauté for about 30 seconds. Add the prosecco and deglaze the pan, scraping up any bits stuck to the pan. Cook for 5 to 6 minutes, until the liquid reduces by a third. Add the bread crumbs and parsley and season to taste with salt and pepper.

4. Return the scallops and any collected juices to the pan and add the extra-virgin olive oil. Toss lightly for 30 to 40 seconds, or until the scallops are heated through and coated with the bread crumbs.

SERVES 6

Note: *Prosecco is an Italian sparkling wine, which you may have to order from the liquor store one or two days ahead of time.*

The flavor of the scallops is enhanced in this dish. Prepare this recipe for a dinner party when you want to serve something fancy and impressive looking. Be sure to buy the freshest scallops available. If you can find them, buy diver scallops that still have the orange "tongue" attached. In Italy, if the scallops are not served with the tongue attached, they are often sent back to the kitchen by customers who insist on impeccable freshness. When scallops cook, they may release a lot of liquid, which can be frustrating for home cooks trying to brown them. The fresher the scallops, the less likely this is to happen. Don't expect much sauce with this dish, just enough to coat the scallops.

Rosanna Scotto's Grilled Veal Chops

¼ cup (60 ml) olive oil
¼ cup (60 ml) balsamic vinegar
6 bone-in veal chops, each 1 to 1¼ inches (2.5 to 3 cm) thick and cut
*   from the rack (4½ to 5 pounds/2 to 2.25 kg total)*
Kosher salt and freshly ground black pepper to taste

1. In a small bowl, combine the oil and vinegar and whisk well.

2. Lay the chops in a glass or ceramic dish and pour the oil and vinegar mixture over them. Cover and refrigerate for at least 1 hour but not longer than 3 hours.

3. Prepare a charcoal or gas grill. The coals should be very hot.

4. Season the chops on both sides with salt and pepper and grill for 4 to 6 minutes on each side for medium. Rotate the chops to make 2 sets of grill marks on the meat. Move the chops to the side of the grill and let them rest for 4 to 5 minutes. Take care not to overcook. Serve immediately.

SERVES 6

Grilled Paillards of Veal

Six 6-ounce (170-g) veal cutlets, pounded thin (use a meat mallet to
*   pound the cutlets or ask the butcher to do it for you)*
3 tablespoons (45 ml) extra-virgin olive oil
Kosher salt and freshly ground black pepper to taste
¼ cup (10 g) chopped fresh herbs such as sage, thyme, and oregano or
*   any combination*

1. Prepare a charcoal or gas grill or preheat the broiler. The coals must be very hot. Charcoal or hardwood will provide the best flavor.

2. Brush both sides of the cutlets with the oil, season to taste with salt and pepper, and sprinkle with the chopped herbs.

3. Grill the cutlets for 1 to 2 minutes on each side. Serve immediately.

SERVES 6

Bistecca Fiorentina
GRILLED STEAK

Six 1½-pound (675-g) T-bone steaks (see Note)
Kosher salt and freshly ground black pepper to taste
2 leafy bunches fresh sage
Extra-virgin olive oil
2 lemons, cut into wedges

1. Prepare a charcoal, wood, or gas grill or preheat the broiler. Let the coals get very hot.

2. Season the steaks with salt and pepper.

3. Divide the sage into 6 small bunches and space them on the grill. Place 1 steak on top of each bunch.

4. Grill for 2 to 3 minutes to a side. When turning the steak, the sage will adhere to the meat. Leave the sage in place when serving.

5. Place each steak on a plate, drizzle with olive oil, and garnish with lemon wedges.

SERVES 6

Note: If possible, buy dry-aged steak, available at fine butchers. It may be difficult to find 1½-pound steaks, in which case, buy two ¾-pound steaks per serving or a couple of large steaks to divide.

As a rule, Italians don't eat large pieces of meat, as we do. Meat is just one course in a three-course meal. This recipe is the exception. When you order Bistecca Fiorentina in Florence, the steak overhangs the plate. During the cooking, branches of fresh sage are laid on the grill and the steak is placed on top of them. If you don't have sage, do not substitute another herb. Go without. Italians use lemon juice on meat to tenderize it because the quality of their meat is not as good as ours. We like the flavor of the lemon, but with good American steak it can be optional.

Top to bottom: Anthony Scotto, Jr.'s Bruschetta with Tomatoes (recipe on page 56); Bistecca Fiorentina

We always have a braised dish or two on the menu, but in the summertime they can be a little heavy. So we came up with these ribs, which are first braised with onions and rosemary until the meat nearly falls from the bone, then grilled for just a few minutes to give them a grilled flavor. We rub a spice mixture on the ribs before grilling but after braising. (If you rubbed it into the raw meat, it would end up in the braising liquid.) The ribs can be braised up to two days ahead of grilling, which makes them a great dish for warm-weather entertaining because essentially they are cooked in advance.

Braised and Grilled Spareribs

1 pound (450 g) onions, julienned
1 head garlic, separated into cloves
6 large sprigs fresh rosemary
2 racks pork spareribs (7 to 8 pounds/3.2 to 3.6 kg)
Kosher salt and freshly ground black pepper to taste
¼ cup (60 ml) olive oil
2 cups (500 ml) Chicken Stock (page 171)
2 cups (500 ml) dry white wine
About ½ cup Fresco Seasoning (page 170)

1. Preheat the oven to 350°F (175°C).

2. In a large roasting pan, arrange the onions, garlic cloves, and rosemary in a single layer.

3. Cut each rack in half so that they will fit into a skillet. Season the ribs with salt and pepper.

4. In a large skillet, heat the olive oil over medium-high heat and sear the ribs for 4 to 6 minutes on each side, until browned. Transfer the ribs to the roasting pan.

5. Add the stock and wine to the roasting pan, cover with aluminum foil, and bake for about 2 hours, until the meat is very tender. Remove the ribs from the pan and strain the pan juices into a saucepan, discarding the solids. Set the pan over medium heat and cook for about 40 minutes, until reduced by half. Season to taste with salt and pepper if necessary. Defat the sauce and set aside, covered, to keep warm.

6. Prepare a charcoal or gas grill so that the coals are very hot.

7. Divide the ribs into 2-rib sections and rub each section with the seasoning mix. Grill for 2 to 3 minutes on each side and serve with the reserved sauce for dipping. Reheat the sauce if necessary; it should be hot.

SERVES 6

Almond Pound Cake with Cherry Sauce

1¼ cups (175 g) cake flour (see Note)
¾ teaspoon baking powder
½ teaspoon salt
9 ounces (260 g) chilled almond paste
1½ cups (310 g) chilled granulated sugar
1¼ cups (280 g) chilled unsalted butter (2½ sticks), cut into pieces
6 large chilled eggs
Cherry Sauce (recipe follows)

1. Preheat the oven to 325°F (165°C). Butter and flour a 9 × 5-inch (23 × 13-cm) loaf pan or an 8-inch (20-cm) round cake pan.

2. In a small bowl, whisk together the flour, baking powder, and salt.

3. In a food processor fitted with a metal blade, combine the almond paste and sugar and pulse 3 to 4 times, or until the mixture forms fine crumbs.

4. Add the butter and pulse 8 to 10 times, until well mixed. Transfer to the bowl of an electric mixer.

5. With the mixer on low speed, add the eggs, one at a time, beating after each addition to incorporate the egg before adding the next one. Mix until the batter is light and fluffy.

6. Using a rubber spatula, fold in the flour mixture. Scrape into the prepared pan and bake on the center rack of the oven for about 1 hour 15 minutes, or until a toothpick inserted in the center comes out clean, the cake begins to pull away from the sides of the pan, and the top is a deep golden brown. Cool completely on a wire rack. Turn out onto a serving plate and serve with Cherry Sauce.

SERVES 6 TO 8

Note: For each cup of cake flour, you can substitute ⅞ cup (1 cup less 2 tablespoons) all-purpose (plain) flour. For this recipe, you would use 1 cup plus 1½ teaspoons (153 g) all-purpose flour.

This pound cake is so versatile, it can be served with almost any flavor ice cream or combination of fruit, but if cherries are in season, they make a delicious sauce. If you go to Italy during cherry season, you will find a sauce similar to this on every menu. It's a simple composition in which the flavor of the cherries really comes through. When making the pound cake, be sure the ingredients are very cold. This goes against many tenets of baking but is absolutely necessary for the success of the cake.

(photograph on page 75)

Opposite, top to bottom:
Raspberry-Fig Tart (recipe page 77),
Almond Pound Cake with Cherry
Sauce (recipe page 73)

Cherry Sauce

¾ cup (150 g) granulated sugar
½ cup (120 ml) dry red wine
One 3-inch (7.5-cm) cinnamon stick
1 tablespoon fresh lemon juice
1 teaspoon finely chopped lemon zest
2 pounds (900 g) fresh cherries, pitted (about 5 cups pitted cherries)

1. In a medium saucepan, combine the sugar, wine, cinnamon stick, lemon juice, and lemon zest. Bring to a boil over high heat and cook for 3 to 4 minutes, until reduced by about one-third.

2. Add the cherries and return to a boil. Immediately remove from the heat and set aside to cool to warm room temperature. Cover and refrigerate for up to 2 days before serving.

MAKES ABOUT 5 CUPS

Note: If you prefer, omit the wine and add more or less sugar, according to personal taste and the natural sweetness of the cherries. However, the lemon, lemon zest, and cinnamon are essential for the sauce.

Serve this refreshingly icy, rich dessert with biscotti or even sweetened whipped cream.

Coconut Lemon Granita

2 cups (500 ml) water
1 cup (250 ml) fresh lemon juice
1 cup (250 ml) cream of coconut
¾ cup (150 g) sugar

1. In a bowl, mix the water, lemon juice, coconut, and sugar until the sugar dissolves. Transfer to a shallow stainless steel pan that fits easily in the freezer. Freeze for about 1 hour. Remove and, with a pastry scraper or metal spatula, scrape the sides and bottom, mixing the frozen particles into the less frozen center.

2. Freeze for about 2 hours longer and scrape again. Let the granita freeze for 3 to 4 hours longer, or until completely frozen. Chop the granita into pieces and serve immediately or return to the freezer until ready to serve.

MAKES ABOUT 2 QUARTS

Fresh Fruit Summer Crisp

FRUIT LAYER

6 cups chopped or whole fresh fruit or berries, such as peaches, plums, apples, strawberries, blueberries (bilberries), raspberries, or blackberries (see Note)
¼ cup (35 g) unbleached all-purpose (plain) flour
¾ cup (150 g) sugar

CRISP TOPPING

6 tablespoons (90 g) unsalted butter, softened
½ cup (100 g) sugar
½ cup (70 g) unbleached all-purpose (plain) flour
1 teaspoon ground cinnamon
½ cup (55 g) chopped nuts, such as walnuts, pecans, hazelnuts (filberts), or almonds

1. Preheat the oven to 375°F (190°C).

2. To prepare the fruit, in a large bowl, combine the fruit with the flour and sugar and stir to mix.

3. To prepare the topping, in an electric mixer set on high speed, beat the butter and sugar for 5 to 6 minutes, until light and fluffy. With the mixer on low speed, add the flour and cinnamon, beating just to incorporate. Do not overmix. Using a wooden spoon, fold the nuts into the batter.

4. In an 8 × 10 × 2-inch (20 × 25 × 5-cm) baking dish, spread the fruit in a single layer. Spoon dollops of the batter over the fruit, flattening them slightly with the back of the spoon and allowing them to overlap slightly. Do not worry if there are gaps in the topping. Bake for about 40 minutes, until the fruit is bubbling and the topping is golden brown. Serve warm or at room temperature.

SERVES 6

Note: Use any combination of fruit you like or use just one kind. For 6 cups you will need approximately 2½ to 3 pounds (1.2 to 1.4 kg) of fruit or 3 pints (1 kg) of berries. Any shallow 2-quart (2-l) baking dish will work here. The topping will keep in the refrigerator for up to 3 days and in the freezer for up to 3 months. Wrap it well in plastic wrap (cling film) and foil.

Raspberry-Fig Tart

1 sheet packaged frozen puff pastry (see Note)
2 cups (325 g) fresh raspberries (about 1 pint)
12 fresh figs, stemmed and quartered
⅓ cup (70 g) sugar
1 large egg

1. Preheat the oven to 375°F (190° C).

2. On a lightly floured surface, roll the pastry sheet into a generous 12-inch (30.5-cm) circle. Do not roll the sheet too thin; it should be just slightly thinner than it is in the package. Transfer to an ungreased baking sheet. Tuck the edges under and, using your fingers or a fork, crimp the edges to make a small rim.

3. Scatter the raspberries over the pastry. Arrange the figs among the raspberries, positioning them so that they are distributed evenly. Sprinkle the sugar over the fruit.

4. In a small bowl, lightly beat the egg with 1 tablespoon of water. Brush the egg wash over the pastry edges. Bake for about 20 minutes, until the crust is lightly browned and the fruit is bubbling and hot. Cool on a wire rack.

SERVES 6

Note: Frozen puff pastry is usually sold in 1-pound (450-g) packages with two sheets to a package. You may want to line the baking sheet with parchment paper, which facilitates moving the tart on and off the baking sheet. Adjust the amount of sugar according to the tartness of the berries.

This tart showcases two of late summer's stars: raspberries and fresh figs. It's quick and easy to make, stunning to look at, and tastes intensely of fresh fruit. You can substitute strawberries or blueberries (bilberries) for the raspberries with equally splendid results. Because the tart relies on commercially available frozen puff pastry, which can be kept on hand in the freezer, you can make it at a moment's notice.
(photograph on page 75)

bread salads

When we were planning Fresco's menus, we wanted to find a way to make our salads a little different from the usual luncheon fare. Vincent suggested putting the same grilled dough he uses for pizza under the greens and then topping it with other salad ingredients. It's a fabulous presentation— very pretty on the plate—and the possibilities for variation are endless. We have included a few of our more popular bread salads, but use your imagination and serve whatever you want—your favorite chicken salad, grilled tuna or steak, or tomato-cucumber salad if you like. The dough must be grilled, so these salads are perfect to make in the summertime when the barbecue is set up. If you have an indoor grill, they easily become a year-round specialty.

Bread Salad with Pepper-Crusted Tuna

Coarsely ground black pepper
2 pounds (900 g) tuna loin (see Note)
1 recipe Fresco Pizza Crust dough (page 162), divided into 6 portions
½ cup (120 ml) extra-virgin olive oil, plus more for brushing on crust
Kosher salt to taste
¼ cup (60 ml) balsamic vinegar
Freshly ground black pepper to taste
10 cups (450 g) mesclun greens (about 1 pound) (see Note)
½ recipe Insalata Rossa (page 44)

1. Prepare a charcoal or gas grill and position the grilling rack 3 to 4 inches (7.5 to 10 cm) above the coals. Let the coals get very hot.

2. Spread the coarsely ground pepper on a flat plate. Press the tuna loin into the pepper so that the pepper adheres to the fish. Grill the tuna, pepper side up, for 1 minute. Turn carefully and grill for 1 minute longer. Remove the tuna from the grill, cover, and set aside in a cool place or refrigerate.

3. On an oiled work surface, flatten 1 dough portion using the palms of your hands. (Leave the remaining 5 portions of dough in a cool place, covered with a damp, well-wrung kitchen towel.) Stretch the dough into a free-form rectangle about 10 by 12 inches (25 by 30 cm) in size. Using your fingertips, drape the dough onto the

grill and cook for 2 to 3 minutes, until the bottom crust is golden brown. Using tongs, flip the crust over and brush with olive oil and sprinkle with salt. Grill for another 2 to 3 minutes, or until the crust is golden brown and crispy. Cover with a dry cloth or foil to keep warm. Repeat with the remaining portions of dough.

4. In a small glass or ceramic bowl, whisk together the ½ cup (120 ml) of olive oil with the vinegar. Season to taste with salt and pepper. In a large mixing bowl, toss the dressing with the greens.

5. Slice the tuna into very thin slices (about ⅓ inch/ 8 mm thick).

6. Using a serrated knife or pizza wheel, cut the grilled bread into wedges and arrange them on 6 plates. Top each wedge with dressed greens and arrange the tuna on each plate. Garnish each plate with about ½ cup of Insalata Rossa and serve immediately.

SERVES 6

Note: Because the tuna is grilled only until it is very rare, buy the best loin tuna you can find from a reputable fishmonger. If possible, buy "sushi-quality" tuna. The tuna may be grilled 3 hours ahead of time, covered, and refrigerated. Slice it just before serving. Grill the tuna longer if you like it more well done.

Mesclun greens are mixed and cleaned tender young greens that include mild and bitter varieties. They are sold packaged or loose in specialty stores, green markets, and many supermarkets. You may substitute your own mixture of greens for mesclun.

Bread Salad with Grilled Shrimp

1½ pounds (675 g) large shrimp (prawns), peeled and deveined
2 tablespoons Fresco Seasoning (page 170)
1 recipe Fresco Pizza Crust dough (page 162), divided into 6 portions
½ cup (190 ml) extra-virgin olive oil, plus more for brushing on crust
Kosher salt to taste
¼ cup (60 ml) balsamic vinegar
Freshly ground black pepper to taste
10 cups (450 g) mesclun greens (about 1 pound) (see Note)
3 cups Corn, Tomato, and Red Onion Salad (¾ recipe, page 55)

1. Prepare a charcoal or gas grill and position the grilling rack 3 to 4 inches (7.5 to 10 cm) above the coals. Let the coals get very hot.

2. In a large bowl, toss the shrimp with the seasoning mix until coated. Thread the shrimp onto metal skewers or arrange them in a single layer in a fine-mesh grilling basket. Cover and refrigerate.

3. On an oiled work surface, flatten 1 dough portion using the palms of your hands. (Leave the remaining 5 portions of dough in a cool place, covered with a damp, well-wrung kitchen towel.) Stretch the dough into a free-form rectangle about 10 by 12 inches (25 by 30 cm) in size. Using your fingertips, drape the dough

(continued on page 80)

5. In a small glass or ceramic bowl, whisk ½ cup (120 ml) of the olive oil with the vinegar. Season to taste with salt and pepper. In a mixing bowl, toss the dressing with the greens.

6. Using a serrated knife or pizza wheel, cut the grilled bread into wedges and arrange them on 6 plates. Top each wedge with dressed greens and arrange shrimp on each plate. Garnish each plate with about ½ cup of corn salad and serve immediately.

SERVES 6

Note: Mesclun greens are mixed and cleaned tender young greens that include mild and bitter varieties. They are sold packaged or loose in specialty stores, green markets, and many supermarkets. You may substitute your own mixture of greens for mesclun.

Bread Salad with Grilled Chicken

Six 6-ounce (170-g) boneless, skinless chicken
   breasts
2 tablespoons Fresco Seasoning (page 170)
1 recipe Fresco Pizza Crust dough (page 162),
   divided into 6 portions
¾ cup (180 ml) extra-virgin olive oil, plus more
   for brushing on crust
Kosher salt to taste
3 large beefsteak tomatoes, cored and cut into
   1-inch chunks

Bread Salad with Grilled Shrimp
(continued from page 79)

onto the grill and cook for 2 to 3 minutes, until the bottom crust is golden brown. Using tongs, flip the crust over and brush with olive oil and sprinkle with salt. Grill for another 2 to 3 minutes, or until the crust is golden brown and crispy. Cover with a dry cloth or foil to keep warm. Repeat with the remaining portions of dough.

4. Grill the shrimp for about 1½ minutes on each side, until pink and opaque. Set aside.

1 cup (115 g) julienned red onions
3 ounces (85 g) fresh mozzarella cheese, cut into
½-inch (1.3-cm) cubes (about 1 cup)
½ cup (20 g) chiffonade of fresh basil
½ cup (120 ml) balsamic vinegar
Freshly ground black pepper to taste
8 cups (340 g) mesclun greens (about ¾ pound)
(see Note)

1. Prepare a charcoal or gas grill and position the grilling rack 3 to 4 inches (7.5 to 10 cm) above the coals. Let the coals get very hot.

2. Season the chicken on both sides with the seasoning mix. Cover and refrigerate.

3. On an oiled work surface, flatten 1 dough portion using the palms of your hands. (Leave the remaining 5 portions of dough in a cool place, covered with a damp, well-wrung kitchen towel.) Stretch the dough into a free-form rectangle about 10 by 12 inches (25 by 30 cm) in size. Using your fingertips, drape the dough onto the grill and cook for 2 to 3 minutes, until the bottom crust is golden brown. Using tongs, flip the crust over and brush with olive oil and sprinkle with salt. Grill for another 2 to 3 minutes, or until the crust is golden brown and crispy. Cover with a dry cloth or foil to keep warm. Repeat with the remaining portions of dough.

4. Grill the chicken for 5 to 6 minutes on each side, until cooked through. Slice each breast into 4 or 5 pieces and set aside.

5. In a large mixing bowl, combine the tomatoes, onions, mozzarella, and basil. Add 6 tablespoons (90 ml) of the olive oil and ¼ cup (60 ml) of the vinegar and toss. Season to taste with salt and pepper.

6. In a small glass or ceramic bowl, whisk together the remaining olive oil and vinegar and season to taste with salt and pepper. In a mixing bowl, toss the dressing with the greens.

7. Using a serrated knife or pizza wheel, cut the grilled bread into wedges and arrange them on 6 plates. Top each wedge with dressed greens and arrange slices of chicken on each plate. Garnish each plate with the tomato salad and serve immediately.

SERVES 6

Note: Mesclun greens are mixed and cleaned tender young greens that include mild and bitter varieties. They are sold packaged or loose in specialty stores, green markets, and many supermarkets. You may substitute your own mixture of greens for mesclun.

We like to serve this as a complete meal with a salad and a loaf of good bread— it's so rich and flavorful. In every restaurant in Italy, the pasta e fagioli is different. Some are thick, some thin, some more of a soup, others more of a pasta dish. When we developed this recipe for the restaurant, we essentially combined Marion Scotto's version with Vincent's—and the result is great. We make the soup with water, not chicken stock, which is typical of the Italian versions. The water emphasizes the flavor of the vegetables. If you would rather use chicken stock, by all means do so for a richer, sharper flavor.

Pasta e Fagioli

1 pound (450 g) dried white beans, such as cannellini or navy, rinsed and
    picked over
¼ cup (60 ml) olive oil
1 tablespoon chopped garlic
½ pound (230 g) carrots, coarsely chopped (about 1⅓ cups)
½ pound (230 g) onions, coarsely chopped (about 1½ cups)
1 bulb fennel, trimmed and coarsely chopped (about 1½ cups)
¼ teaspoon crushed red pepper flakes, or to taste
2 tablespoons chopped fresh rosemary
¼ pound (115 g) prosciutto in one piece
4 quarts (4 l) water, or 3 quarts (3 l) water and 1 quart (1 l) Chicken
    Stock (page 171)
¼ teaspoon salt, or to taste
Freshly ground black pepper to taste
1 pound (450 g) dried tubettini pasta
¾ cup (85 g) freshly grated Parmesan cheese

1. Put the beans in a large pot and add enough cold water to cover by 2 to 3 inches (5 to 7.5 cm). Set aside to soak overnight or for 6 to 8 hours. Drain, rinse the beans with fresh water, and drain again (see Note).

2. In a large pot, heat the oil over medium heat, add the garlic, and cook for 2 to 3 minutes, or until soft and golden. Add the carrots, onions, fennel, red pepper flakes, and rosemary and cook, uncovered, for 20 to 25 minutes, or until the vegetables are very tender.

3. Add the beans, prosciutto, and water. Bring to a boil, reduce the heat to a simmer, and cook, uncovered, for 1 to 1½ hours, or until the beans are very tender.

4. Lift the prosciutto from the pot, trim off the fat, and set aside.

5. Ladle 1½ cups (375 ml) of the soup, both solids and broth, into a food processor fitted with the metal blade and puree. Return to the pot. Put the prosciutto in the food processor and pulse until finely chopped. Return to the pot. Season to taste with salt and pepper.

6. In a large pot of lightly salted boiling water, cook the pasta for 8 to 10 minutes, or until al dente. Drain, reserving 1 cup (250 ml) of the pasta water.

7. Add the pasta to the beans and vegetables and stir over high heat for 1½ to 2 minutes to allow the pasta to combine with the sauce. If the mixture is too thick, add the reserved pasta water as needed until it is the consistency of thick soup.

8. Garnish generously with grated cheese (about 2 tablespoons per serving) and serve.

SERVES 6

Note: *To prepare the beans by the quick-soak method, put the beans in a large pot and add enough cold water to cover by 2 to 3 inches (5 to 7.5 cm). Bring to a boil over high heat and cook for 2 minutes. Remove from the heat and set aside for 1 hour. Proceed with the recipe.*

The carrots, onions, and fennel can be processed in a food processor fitted with a metal blade until coarsely chopped. For a meat-free dish, omit the prosciutto.

Red Bean and Farro Soup

¼ cup (60 ml) olive oil
1⅓ cups (160 g) finely diced onions (about 2½ onions)
1⅓ cups (160 g) finely diced fennel (about 1 bulb)
2 teaspoons chopped fresh garlic (about 4 cloves)
2 teaspoons crushed red pepper flakes, or to taste
½ pound (230 g) dried red kidney beans, rinsed and picked over (see Note)
2 tablespoons chopped fresh rosemary
¼ pound (115 g) prosciutto in 1 piece or 1 ham hock (see Note)
1 cup (250 ml) tomato puree
Salt to taste
⅔ cup (115 g) farro or barley
Freshly grated Parmesan cheese, for garnish (optional)

1. In a large pot, heat the olive oil over medium heat. Add the onions, fennel, garlic, and red pepper flakes and sauté for about 15 minutes, until the vegetables soften.

(continued on page 86)

Pages 82–83, left to right: Sausage and Leek Tart with Fennel Crust (recipe on page 112), White Bean–Sweet Potato Soup (recipe on page 86), Savory Greens with Orange Vinaigrette (recipe on page 87)

Here is another soup that is found on the menu in nearly every restaurant in Tuscany and is a little different in each one. Farro is a grain that grows wild in Italy, but if you can't find it, substitute barley, which works very well. It's hard to surpass this combination of grain and beans for full flavor and hearty texture.

(continued from page 85)

2. Add 4 quarts (4 l) of water and the kidney beans, rosemary, prosciutto, tomato puree, and salt. Bring to a boil, reduce the heat to medium, and simmer, uncovered, for about 1 hour 20 minutes.

3. Add the farro and cook for about 30 minutes more, until tender. Season with salt if necessary.

4. Remove the prosciutto from the pot. When cool enough to handle, trim and discard the fat and finely chop the meat. Return the meat to the pan, heat gently until hot, and serve, garnished with grated Parmesan if desired.

SERVES 6

Note: The kidney beans do not require soaking before cooking. If you use a ham hock, buy it smoked or not, depending on availability and personal preference.

White Bean–Sweet Potato Soup

¼ cup (60 ml) olive oil
¼ pound (115 g) pancetta, finely diced (about ½ cup)
3 carrots, finely diced (about 1 cup)
1 onion, finely diced (about 1 cup)
1 small bulb fennel, trimmed and finely diced (about 1 cup)
2 tablespoons chopped garlic
1 pound (450 g) dried navy beans, rinsed and picked over
2 tablespoons chopped fresh rosemary
1 teaspoon kosher salt, plus more for seasoning
1 teaspoon crushed red pepper flakes
3 quarts (3 l) Chicken Stock (page 171)
3 sweet potatoes, peeled and cut into ⅓-inch (8-mm) cubes
  (about 4 cups)
½ cup (55 g) freshly grated Parmesan cheese

1. In a large stockpot, heat the olive oil over medium-low heat. Add the pancetta and cook, uncovered, for 20 to 30 minutes, until the fat is rendered.

2. Add the carrots, onion, fennel, garlic, beans, rosemary, salt, red pepper flakes, stock, and 4 to 6 cups (1 to 1.5 l) water. Bring to a boil, reduce the heat

You won't find a soup in Italy that includes both sweet potatoes and white beans; sweet potatoes are not native tubers and are rarely eaten there. Nevertheless, this soup is representative of our modern Tuscan style of cooking because we add rosemary and pancetta, two flavors often found in Tuscany. The result is a warming late-fall treat that is equally welcome throughout the rest of the cold months.

(photograph on page 83)

to medium, and simmer for about 1 hour, uncovered, or until the beans are cooked al dente.

3. Add the sweet potatoes and Parmesan cheese and continue to simmer for about 20 minutes, or until the potatoes are tender and the beans are soft.

4. Ladle 3 cups (750 ml) of the soup, both solids and broth, into a food processor fitted with the metal blade and puree. Return to the pot and heat through.

5. Season with additional salt if necessary, and serve.

SERVES 6 TO 8

Note: This soup tastes best when it's made a day in advance. It can be frozen for up to 2 months.

Savory Greens with Orange Vinaigrette

We like to serve this salad in the autumn with *Sausage and Leek Tart with Fennel Crust.*
(photograph on page 83)

VINAIGRETTE
1 cup (250 ml) fresh orange juice
1 tablespoon mashed garlic
Kosher salt and freshly ground black pepper to taste
½ cup (120 ml) extra-virgin olive oil

SALAD
1 medium bulb fennel
1 head frisee (see Note)
2 heads Belgium endive (witloof)
Kosher salt and freshly ground black pepper to taste
6 tablespoons toasted sliced almonds

1. To make the dressing, in a small saucepan, heat the orange juice over medium heat and simmer for 5 to 6 minutes, until reduced to ¼ cup (60 ml) and thickened to a syrupy consistency. Transfer to a mixing bowl and let cool slightly.

2. Add the garlic to the orange juice and whisk to mix. Season to taste with salt and pepper. Slowly add the olive oil to the orange juice, whisking constantly

(continued on page 88)

until the dressing is emulsified and thick. Use immediately or cover and refrigerate. Whisk well before using.

3. To assemble the salad, shave the fennel bulb into thin shavings and drop into acidulated water (see Note). Tear the frisee into pieces and separate the endive leaves and place in a serving bowl. Drain the fennel and add to the bowl. Toss with the dressing and adjust the seasonings with salt and pepper. Sprinkle with the almonds and serve.

SERVES 6

Note: The vinaigrette can be prepared up to 3 days in advance, covered, and refrigerated. Frisee is also known as curly endive (escarole). Acidulated water is made by adding a small amount of an acidic ingredient such as lemon juice or vinegar to cool water. It prevents discoloration in vegetables and fruits that tend to turn brown when exposed to the air upon cutting.

Focaccia with Robiola Cheese

When traveling in Italy, we stopped in Santa Margarita, a beautiful coastal town on the Italian Riviera. Restaurants there commonly serve robiola cheese, using it to make focaccias or pizzas, baking them right in front of you in brick ovens and bringing them to the table dripping with this tangy, creamy cheese. We developed this version, which we serve warm or at room temperature as an appetizer or an accompaniment to salad. If necessary, substitute dry ricotta.

Cornmeal (maize flour), for dusting
Unbleached all-purpose (plain) flour, for rolling the dough
1 recipe Fresco Pizza Crust dough (page 162), divided in half
¾ pound (340 g) fresh robiola cheese or dry ricotta (see Note)
2 teaspoons olive oil
1 teaspoon coarsely chopped fresh rosemary
Kosher salt to taste

1. Preheat the oven to 350°F (175°C). Dust a baking sheet with cornmeal.

2. On a work surface lightly dusted with flour, roll half of the dough into a 10-inch (25-cm) round. (This does not have to be a perfect circle.) Transfer to the baking sheet. Sprinkle more flour on the work surface if necessary, and roll the second half into a 10-inch round and set aside.

3. Dollop the cheese over the first round of dough and spread it evenly, leaving a ¼-inch (6-mm) border. Sprinkle a tablespoon of water over the cheese. Using a brush, brush another tablespoon of water along the border. Lay the

Opposite, top to bottom:
Focaccia with Robiola Cheese;
Penne with Green Tomato Sauce
(recipe on page 97)

(continued on page 90)

Focaccia with Robiola Cheese
(continued from page 88)

second round of dough over the cheese and, using your thumb and forefinger, press the 2 rounds together to seal the dough.

4. Brush the top of the focaccia with olive oil and sprinkle with rosemary and salt. Bake for 20 to 25 minutes on the center rack of the oven, until both the top and bottom of the focaccia are browned. Cut the focaccia into wedges and serve hot or at room temperature.

SERVES 6

Note: If you cannot buy dry ricotta, available at some Italian markets and specialty stores, drain ordinary ricotta in a cheesecloth-lined colander for at least 4 hours. When using ricotta, you may not need to sprinkle the cheese with water, as it will already be quite moist. When you cut the ricotta-filled focaccia for serving, it will appear wet but will firm up as it cools slightly.

Three-Cheese Pesto Ravioli with Walnut-Butter Sauce

RAVIOLI
2 cups (200 g) freshly grated Parmesan cheese
2 cups (230 g) grated fresh whole-milk mozzarella cheese
1 cup (230 g) fresh ricotta cheese
¼ cup (55 g) Pesto (page 167)
2 tablespoons chopped fresh flat-leaf parsley
Kosher salt and freshly ground black pepper to taste
2 large eggs, lightly beaten
*Sixty 2½-inch (6.4-cm) fresh pasta squares or wonton wrappers
    (about 1 pound/450 g; see Note)*

SAUCE
1 cup (2 sticks/230 g) unsalted butter
Kosher salt and freshly ground black pepper to taste
1 cup (115 g) chopped toasted walnuts
1 cup (115 g) freshly grated Parmesan cheese

1. To assemble the ravioli, in a bowl, combine the cheeses, pesto, parsley, and salt and pepper to taste and mix well. Add the eggs and mix again so that the filling is cohesive. (You will have about 3¾ cups of filling.)

2. On a work surface, lay out a pasta square or wonton wrapper and spoon 1 generous tablespoon (about 1 ounce/30 g) of filling onto the center. Using your fingertips or a brush, dampen the edges of the pasta with cold water and lay a second square on top. Press the edges together, using your fingertips or a fork to crimp the edges of the ravioli closed, pressing out any trapped air in the process, and making sure to form a tight seal. If necessary, dab a little more water on the pasta to ensure a tight seal. Set aside on a baking sheet or tray and cover with a damp, well-wrung kitchen towel. Continue with the remaining filling and pasta to make 30 ravioli. Arrange the ravioli in a single layer on the baking sheet so that they do not stick together.

3. Bring a large pot of lightly salted water to a boil and, using a slotted spoon or spatula, submerge 5 or 6 ravioli in the water and cook for about 5 minutes, until al dente. Using a slotted spoon, lift the ravioli from the water, let drain, and set on a warm serving platter. Hold the platter in a warm (200°F/95°C) oven while cooking all the ravioli. Let the water return to a boil between batches. After all the ravioli are cooked, reserve ½ cup (120 ml) of the pasta cooking water.

4. To prepare the sauce, in a large skillet, melt the butter over medium heat and season to taste with salt and pepper. Add the reserved pasta cooking water and simmer for 2 minutes. Spoon the sauce over the ravioli on the serving platter, taking care to cover all the ravioli. Sprinkle with walnuts and cheese and serve immediately.

SERVES 6

Note: Fresh pasta sheets are often sold in specialty stores or Italian markets. Wonton wrappers, which are an acceptable substitute, are readily available in supermarkets.

This is another idea from Santa Margarita, where ravioli is a traditional dish. We use our usual three-cheese mixture of mozzarella, ricotta, and Parmesan, which we mix with a little pesto. Although pesto is rich, its flavors actually lighten the cheese mixture. There is no need to top these ravioli with a tomato sauce—the cheeses and pesto provide enough play of flavors. Instead, they are nicely enhanced by a simple butter-walnut sauce.

Nothing can beat this for a perfect autumn dish in which the sweetness of the squash offsets the salty pancetta. Italians don't cook with butternut squash, which is an American vegetable, although they make a lasagne somewhat similar to this with their version of "pumpkin"—which does not resemble American pumpkin but is a squashlike vegetable.

Butternut Squash and Pancetta Lasagne

BÉCHAMEL SAUCE
3 cups (750 ml) milk
1 shallot, coarsely chopped
¼ teaspoon freshly grated nutmeg
4½ tablespoons (70 g) unsalted butter
4½ tablespoons (40 g) unbleached all-purpose (plain) flour
Salt to taste

LASAGNE
3 tablespoons (45 g) unsalted butter
6 tablespoons (90 ml) olive oil
8 cups (900 g) julienned onions (about 2 pounds)
Salt and freshly ground black pepper to taste
One 3-pound (1.4-kg) butternut (winter) squash, peeled and cut into
    ½-inch (1.3-cm) cubes
1 pound (450 g) pancetta, chopped
2 cups (280 g) diced fresh whole-milk mozzarella cheese
1 cup (230 g) fresh ricotta cheese
3 cups (300 g) freshly grated Parmesan cheese (about 11 ounces)
2 large eggs
¼ cup (10 g) chopped fresh flat-leaf parsley
1 pound (450 g) fresh pasta sheets or 8 ounces (230 g) dried lasagne sheets
½ cup (120 ml) heavy (double) cream

1. To make the béchamel sauce, combine 2½ cups (630 ml) of the milk, the shallot, and nutmeg in a small saucepan and bring to a boil over medium heat. Reduce the heat and simmer, uncovered, for about 5 minutes. Cover and set aside to keep hot.

2. In another saucepan, melt the butter over medium-low heat. Add the flour and, using a wooden spoon, stir until the flour absorbs the butter and forms a roux. Continue stirring for 2 to 3 minutes longer while the mixture bubbles and thickens.

3. Slowly pour the hot milk into the flour, whisking continuously to prevent lumps. Bring the sauce to a boil over medium heat. Reduce the heat and simmer for 2 to 3 minutes, until smooth and thickened. Season to taste with salt.

4. Strain through a fine sieve into a bowl or glass measuring cup. Add as much of the remaining ½ cup (120 ml) milk as necessary to make 2½ cups (630 ml), whisking well to incorporate. Set aside, covered, until ready to use (see Note).

5. To prepare the lasagne, in a large skillet, heat the butter and 3 tablespoons of the oil over medium heat until the butter melts. Add the onions and cook, stirring often, for about 45 minutes, until softened and beginning to caramelize. Season to taste with salt and set aside until ready to use.

6. Preheat the oven to 350°F (175°C).

7. In a bowl, toss the squash with the remaining 3 tablespoons of oil and season to taste with salt and pepper. Spread the squash on a baking sheet in a single layer and bake for about 1 hour, until fork-tender and golden brown around the edges. Set aside to cool. When cool, combine with the onions.

8. In a large skillet, cook the pancetta over low heat, uncovered, for 25 to 30 minutes, until it is browned and the fat is rendered. Drain and discard the fat. Set the pancetta aside to cool.

9. In a small bowl, combine the mozzarella, ricotta, 2 cups (200 g) of the Parmesan, the eggs, and parsley. Stir well and season to taste with salt and pepper.

10. If using dried lasagne, bring a large pot of lightly salted water to a boil and cook the pasta for 8 to 10 minutes, until barely al dente. Drain and separate the sheets to cool. If using fresh pasta, do not cook it before assembling the lasagne.

11. In a 9 × 13-inch (23 × 33-cm) baking pan that is at least 2 inches (5 cm) deep, spread the cream over the bottom, tilting the pan if necessary to spread evenly. Lay a quarter of the lasagne sheets over the cream, overlapping slightly and trimming if necessary to fit.

12. Spread a third of the cheese mixture evenly over the pasta. Top with a third of the squash and onions and a third of the pancetta. Drizzle ¾ cup (180 ml) of the béchamel sauce over the pancetta. Top with a quarter of the lasagne sheets.

(continued on page 94)

Repeat the process, ending with the pasta sheets and pressing down to compress the layers slightly. Pour the remaining béchamel evenly over the pasta and sprinkle with the remaining 1 cup (100 g) of Parmesan.

13. Bake, uncovered, for about 1 hour, until the top is golden brown and the sides are bubbling. Let stand 10 to 15 minutes before serving.

SERVES 6 TO 8

Note: The béchamel sauce and the cheese, squash and onion, and pancetta fillings can be prepared and refrigerated, covered, for up to 2 days in advance. Before using the chilled béchamel, thin it slightly by whisking in 3 to 4 tablespoons (50 to 60 ml) of milk if necessary.

Here's another Italian American dish we all grew up with in Brooklyn. It's one of the simplest pasta dishes to make, and because lentils cook quickly, you can have a robust fall meal relatively quickly. Serve this with a loaf of bread and a salad for an extremely satisfying meal.

Rigatoni with a Ragù of Lentils

¼ cup (60 ml) olive oil
1 cup (115 g) finely chopped carrots
1 cup (115 g) finely chopped onions
1 cup (115 g) finely chopped fennel
2 tablespoons chopped garlic
1 pound (450 g) dried brown lentils, rinsed
3 cups (750 ml) water
2 cups (500 ml) tomato puree
¼ cup (10 g) chopped fresh flat-leaf parsley
1 tablespoon chopped fresh rosemary
1 teaspoon crushed red pepper flakes
Kosher salt to taste
1½ pounds (675 g) dried rigatoni pasta
½ cup (55 g) freshly grated Parmesan cheese

1. In a large saucepan or Dutch oven, heat the oil over medium heat. Add the carrots, onions, fennel, and garlic and cook, covered, for about 25 minutes, until the vegetables soften.

2. Add the lentils, water, tomato puree, parsley, rosemary, and red pepper flakes. Cook for 30 minutes, covered, and until the lentils begin to soften. Season to taste with salt. Cook for 10 to 15 minutes more, or until the lentils are tender.

3. Bring a large pot of lightly salted water to a boil and cook the pasta for 8 to 10 minutes, or until al dente. Drain, add to the lentil ragù, and toss gently for 1 to 2 minutes over high heat, until the pasta is hot and coated with the sauce from the ragù. Toss with the cheese and serve.

SERVES 6

Rigatoni with Cauliflower and Bread Crumbs

1½ pounds (675 g) dried rigatoni, mezzani, or other large tubular pasta
3 cups (260 g) cauliflower florets (about 9 ounces)
½ cup (120 ml) olive oil
2 large cloves garlic, chopped
1 tablespoon crushed red pepper flakes
2 tablespoons chopped fresh flat-leaf parsley
Salt to taste
¾ cup (115 g) toasted fine bread crumbs

1. Bring a large pot of lightly salted water to a boil and cook the pasta and cauliflower florets for about 4 minutes, until both are barely al dente. Drain, reserving 1 cup (250 ml) of the cooking water.

2. In large sauté pan, heat the olive oil over medium heat. Add the garlic and sauté for about 1 minute, until golden. Add the red pepper flakes and parsley and season to taste with salt.

3. Add the pasta, cauliflower, and reserved pasta cooking water to the pan and cook over medium-high heat for about 3 minutes, until the water is reduced by half and the pasta is al dente.

4. Remove the pan from the heat, add ½ cup (70 g) of the bread crumbs, and toss. Transfer to a serving platter and garnish with the remaining ¼ cup (45 g) of bread crumbs.

SERVES 6

This peasant-style dish is not only easy to make but can be served in 10 minutes. The rigatoni and cauliflower are cooked in the same pot and then mixed with a basic oil and garlic sauce. Once you make this several times, you can experiment with it—for example, by substituting broccoli for the cauliflower or adding some anchovies and chopped walnuts, two prevalent flavors in Tuscany. Note that bread crumbs are used in place of grated cheese, which is a clue to the modest roots of this dish.

No doubt about it, this is one of the richest dishes we serve at the restaurant. Initially we did not want pastas with heavy cream sauces on the menu, but later decided that because some of our customers like them, we would develop a very simple one. Since the day we first offered it, this has been universally popular. We like to serve it as an appetizer because it is so rich, although we have customers who often order it as an entree. We like to make this at home too, since it can be prepared ahead of time, which means we can get out of the kitchen once the guests arrive.

Penne Gratin

¼ pound (115 g) pancetta, diced (about ¾ cup)
1 pound (450 g) dried penne
¼ cup (60 g) unsalted butter
4 cups (400 g) freshly grated Parmesan cheese (about 14 ounces)
¾ cup (180 ml) heavy (double) cream
1 teaspoon cracked black pepper

1. In a skillet, cook the pancetta over medium-low heat, partially covered, for about 45 minutes, until the fat is rendered. (You will have about ¼ cup/60 ml.)

2. Bring a large pot of lightly salted water to a boil and cook the pasta for 10 to 12 minutes, until barely al dente. Drain and cover to keep warm.

3. Preheat the broiler (griller).

4. In a large saucepan or large, deep skillet, heat the butter over medium-high heat. Add the pancetta, 3 cups (300 g) of the Parmesan cheese, the cream, and pepper. Bring to a simmer and cook, stirring constantly, just until the cheese melts. Add the drained pasta and toss.

5. Transfer the pasta mixture to a shallow 12 × 14-inch (30.5 × 35.5-cm) broiler-safe dish, spreading it evenly. Top evenly with the remaining 1 cup (100 g) Parmesan cheese. Broil (grill) for 3 to 4 minutes, until browned.

SERVES 6

Note: If you prefer, omit the pancetta for a meat-free dish.

Penne with Green Tomato Sauce

½ cup (120 ml) olive oil
1½ tablespoons chopped garlic
2 pounds (900 g) large green tomatoes, seeded and chopped into ¼-inch
    (6-mm) pieces (about 4 cups; see Note)
1 teaspoon crushed red pepper flakes
1 teaspoon salt, plus more to taste
¼ cup (10 g) chopped fresh basil
1 pound (450 g) dried penne pasta
2 tablespoons unsalted butter, softened
Freshly grated Parmesan cheese, for garnish

1. In a large saucepan, heat the oil over medium-high heat. Add the garlic and sauté for about 1 minute, or until golden brown.

2. Add the tomatoes, red pepper flakes, and 1 teaspoon of salt and cook, stirring often, for 15 to 20 minutes, until the tomatoes soften enough to make a lumpy sauce. Add the basil and more salt if necessary.

3. Meanwhile, bring a large pot of lightly salted water to a boil and cook the pasta for 6 to 8 minutes, until barely al dente. Drain, reserving 1 cup (250 ml) of the cooking water.

4. Add the pasta and reserved cooking water to the sauce and cook for 2 to 3 minutes, until the sauce adheres to pasta. Add the butter and toss briefly to coat the pasta. Season with more salt if necessary.

5. Transfer to a serving platter and garnish with Parmesan cheese.

SERVES 6

Note: For best results, use large, firm, fleshy green tomatoes. Small tomatoes have tougher skins, and their size makes it difficult to separate the seeds from the flesh.

Green tomato sauce is common in Italy, but we developed this recipe because of the large numbers of green tomatoes we found in our regular fresh tomato order in the early fall. Green tomato sauce is more acidic than red, but it has a great fresh taste. Most of the time, we just toss the simple sauce with pasta, but we sometimes add roasted vegetables for pasta primavera without the cream. In Italy cooks sometimes add diced green and red bell peppers. Make a big batch of the sauce and freeze it in small containers so that through the winter you can experience a little bite of late summer.

(photograph on page 89)

Pappardelle with Veal Ragù and Pumpkin

During our travels in Italy, we spent a lot of time in Florence, where, as throughout all of Tuscany, meat sauces with vibrant flavors are typical. We learned that there is never a lot of sauce on the plate because the sauce is cooked for so long that its flavors intensify to such a degree that you need only a small amount. This method of making ragù was developed years ago as a way to stretch a small amount of meat when money was tight. In this recipe the long cooking takes place in step 1. Patience is in order—and it's worth it.

½ cup (120 ml) plus 1 tablespoon olive oil
1½ cups (170 g) finely chopped onions
1 cup (115 g) finely chopped carrots
1 cup (115 g) finely chopped fennel
3 to 4 large cloves garlic, chopped (about 2 tablespoons)
1½ teaspoons kosher salt
½ teaspoon crushed red pepper flakes
¾ pound (340 g) pumpkin or butternut (winter) squash, cut in ½-inch (1.3-cm) cubes (about 3 cups)
1 pound (450 g) veal stew meat, cut in ⅓-inch (8-mm) cubes
1 cup (250 ml) dry red wine
1 cup (250 ml) Veal Stock (page 171), or ½ cup (120 ml) Chicken Stock (page 171) and ½ cup Beef Stock (page 171)
1½ pounds (675 g) dried pappardelle or other wide noodles (see Note)
½ cup (120 ml) milk
½ cup (120 ml) tomato puree
¼ cup (60 g) unsalted butter
6 large fresh basil leaves, optional
Freshly grated Parmesan cheese

1. In a large, heavy-bottomed pot, heat ½ cup (120 ml) of the oil over low heat. Add the onions, carrots, fennel, garlic, 1 teaspoon of the salt, and the red pepper flakes. Cook, uncovered, for about 45 minutes, stirring occasionally, until very soft.

2. Meanwhile, preheat the oven to 350°F (175°C).

3. In a large bowl, toss the pumpkin with the remaining 1 tablespoon of olive oil and remaining ½ teaspoon of salt.

4. Spread the pumpkin in a shallow roasting pan or baking sheet and bake for about 30 minutes, until tender and brown around the edges. Remove from the pan and set aside. If necessary, use a spatula to loosen any pumpkin cubes sticking to the roasting pan.

5. Add the veal to the pot with the vegetables, raise the heat to medium, and cook, uncovered, for 3 to 4 minutes, until the meat loses its pink color.

6. Add the wine and stock and simmer for about 30 minutes, until most of the liquid has evaporated.

7. Bring a large pot of lightly salted water to a boil and cook the pasta for 6 to 8 minutes, until barely al dente. Drain and keep warm.

8. Meanwhile, add the milk to the veal ragù and cook for 10 to 15 minutes, until most of the liquid has evaporated. Add the tomato puree and cook for 10 more minutes, until slightly thickened.

9. Add the pasta to the veal ragù and toss over medium heat for 1 minute, or until heated through.

10. Add the roasted pumpkin and the butter. Toss until the butter melts. Stir in the basil leaves. Serve with Parmesan cheese.

SERVES 6

Note: Pappardelle is 1 inch (2.5 cm) wide, making it the widest pasta noodle. It is available in some supermarkets, in Italian groceries, and in specialty stores.

Risotto with Garlic Sausage, Tomatoes, and Arugula

½ pound (230 g) cotechino (garlic) sausage
5 cups (1.2 l) Chicken Stock (page 171)
6 tablespoons (90 ml) olive oil
5 whole cloves garlic
2 cups (340 g) arborio or carnaroli rice
⅓ cup (80 ml) dry white wine
¼ pound (115 g) arugula (rocket) leaves, coarsely chopped
    (about 2 loosely packed cups)
4 plum (egg) tomatoes, seeded and finely diced
½ cup (55 g) freshly grated Parmesan cheese

For a true risotto, you never stop stirring the rice until all the liquid is incorporated. The liquid must be added in small amounts to provide enough friction during stirring so that the outer hulls of the rice wear off, leaving a chewy center and, at the same time, creating a creamy consistency.

(continued on page 100)

(continued on page 100)

Risotto with Garlic Sausage,
Tomatoes, and Arugula
(continued from page 99)

Kosher salt and freshly ground black pepper to taste
1 tablespoon brandy
2 tablespoons chopped fresh flat-leaf parsley
3 tablespoons (45 ml) extra-virgin olive oil

Vincent likes to use carnaroli rice, although any medium-grain rice, such as arborio, results in excellent risotto. It is important to use a medium-grain rice to produce the proper consistency. Some risotto recipes call for the addition of butter and cream at the end of cooking to make them smooth and creamy, but no authentic risotto includes these ingredients. The key to the creaminess is in the stirring. For this recipe, try to use garlic sausage; there really is no substitute.

1. Place the sausage in a large saucepan and add enough cold water to cover by 1 inch (2.5 cm). Bring to a simmer over medium-high heat and cook for about 10 minutes. Remove from the water and, when cool enough to handle, remove the casing and chop coarsely. Set aside.

2. In another large saucepan, bring the stock to a simmer over medium-high heat. Reduce the heat to medium or medium-low to keep the liquid barely simmering.

3. In a large, heavy stockpot, heat the olive oil over medium heat. Add the garlic and cook for 3 to 5 minutes, until golden brown. Using a slotted spoon, remove the garlic from the oil and discard.

4. Raise the heat to medium-high, add the rice, and stir for about 15 seconds, or until the grains are well coated with oil.

5. Add the wine and stir constantly, being careful to scrape the sides and bottom of the pan gently so that the rice does not stick. When the wine is almost gone, add ½ cup (120 ml) of the simmering stock and stir until the stock is nearly absorbed by the rice. Repeat, adding ½ cup (120 ml) of the stock after each preceding amount has been almost absorbed, until all the stock is used. The entire process will take 17 or 18 minutes. It is very important to stir the rice constantly for even cooking and a creamy texture, although it will remain al dente.

6. When all the broth has been used, add the sausage, arugula, tomatoes, and cheese, stirring gently to mix. Cook for about 3 minutes, or until the flavors blend. Season with salt and pepper to taste.

7. Remove from the heat and add the brandy. Stir vigorously for 30 seconds to incorporate the brandy. Divide the risotto among 6 plates and garnish each one with chopped parsley and a drizzle of extra-virgin olive oil.

SERVES 6

Risotto with Wild Mushrooms

2 ounces (55 g) dried porcini mushrooms
2 tablespoons unsalted butter
¾ pound (340 g) fresh wild mushrooms, such as oysters, shiitakes, or
*   chanterelles, wiped clean, trimmed, and sliced*
Salt and freshly ground black pepper to taste
4 cups (1 l) Chicken Stock (page 171)
6 tablespoons (90 ml) olive oil
5 large whole cloves garlic
2 cups (340 g) arborio or carnaroli rice
⅓ cup (80 ml) dry white wine
½ cup (55 g) freshly grated Parmesan cheese
3 tablespoons chopped fresh flat-leaf parsley
1 tablespoon brandy

1. In a bowl, pour 1 cup (250 ml) of boiling water over the dried mushrooms and set aside for about 20 minutes to rehydrate.

2. In a large sauté pan, melt the butter over medium heat. Add the fresh mushrooms and cook, covered, for 3 to 5 minutes, or until the mushrooms begin to release their liquid. Season to taste with salt and pepper.

3. Put the stock into a large saucepan.

4. Remove the mushrooms from the heat and drain any released liquid into the chicken stock. Set the mushrooms aside.

5. Drain the porcini mushrooms, straining and reserving their soaking liquid. (There should be about ½ cup/120 ml of liquid.) Finely chop the porcini. Add the strained soaking liquid into the chicken stock.

6. Bring the stock to a simmer over medium-high heat. Reduce the heat to medium or medium-low to keep the liquid barely simmering.

7. In a large, heavy stockpot, heat the olive oil over medium heat. Add the garlic and cook for 3 to 5 minutes, until golden brown. Using a slotted spoon, remove the garlic from the oil and discard.

8. Raise the heat to medium-high, add the rice, and stir for about 15 seconds, or until the grains are well coated with oil.

(continued on page 103)

Many supermarkets and specialty stores across the country carry excellent selections of cultivated "wild" mushrooms, which are absolutely terrific in risotto. While it's a nice idea to mix two or three types of mushrooms, we don't use more than that. Otherwise the flavors could get lost.

9. Add the wine and porcini and stir constantly, being careful to scrape the sides and bottom of the pan gently so that the rice does not stick. When the wine is almost gone, add ½ cup (120 ml) of the simmering stock, stirring until the stock is nearly absorbed by the rice. Repeat, adding ½ cup (120 ml) of the stock after each preceding amount has been almost absorbed, until all the stock is used. The entire process will take 17 or 18 minutes. It is very important to stir the rice constantly for even cooking and a creamy texture, although it will remain al dente.

10. When all the broth has been used, add the fresh mushrooms, Parmesan, and parsley, stirring gently to mix. Cook for about 3 minutes, or until the flavors blend. Season with salt and pepper to taste.

11. Remove from the heat and add the brandy. Stir vigorously for 30 seconds to incorporate the brandy. Divide the risotto among 6 plates.

SERVES 6

Risotto with Chicken, Mushrooms, and Spinach

5 cups (1.2 l) Chicken Stock (page 171)
2 tablespoons unsalted butter
¾ pound (340 g) white mushrooms, thinly sliced (about 4 cups)
6 tablespoons (90 ml) olive oil
5 whole cloves garlic
1 cup (115 g) finely diced onions
2 cups (340 g) arborio or carnaroli rice
⅓ cup (80 ml) dry white wine
½ pound (230 g) roasted chicken meat, cut into small pieces (about 2 cups)
3 cups (130 g) loosely packed coarsely chopped fresh spinach leaves
½ cup (55 g) freshly grated Parmesan cheese
Kosher salt and freshly ground black pepper to taste

Risotto with Wild Mushrooms
(continued from page 101)

Opposite, left to right: Risotto with Wild Mushrooms (recipe on page 101); Fillet of Snapper with Tomatoes, Olives, and Roasted Potatoes (recipe on page 105)

The combination of chicken, mushrooms, and spinach is an appealing one, particularly when stirred into creamy risotto. While ordinary button mushrooms work very well here, you could substitute your favorite wild mushrooms instead. We use roasted chicken for the combination of white and dark meat, but you could use chicken cutlets.

(continued on page 104)

1 tablespoon brandy
2 tablespoons chopped fresh flat-leaf parsley
3 tablespoons (45 ml) extra-virgin olive oil

1. In a large saucepan, bring the stock to a simmer over medium-high heat. Reduce the heat to medium or medium-low to keep the liquid barely simmering.

2. In a large sauté pan, melt the butter over medium heat. Add the mushrooms, cover, and cook for 4 to 5 minutes, until the mushrooms soften and release most of their liquid. Do not brown. Remove the mushrooms from the pan and set aside.

3. In a large, heavy stockpot, heat the olive oil over medium heat. Add the garlic and cook for 3 to 5 minutes, until golden brown. Using a slotted spoon, remove the garlic from the oil and discard. Add the onions and sauté for 10 to 12 minutes, covered, until they soften and turn slightly golden.

4. Raise the heat to medium-high, add the rice, and stir for about 15 seconds, or until the grains are well coated with oil.

5. Add the wine and stir constantly, being careful to scrape the sides and bottom of the pan gently so that the rice does not stick. When the wine is almost gone, add ½ cup (120 ml) of the simmering stock and stir until the stock is nearly absorbed by the rice. Repeat, adding ½ cup (120 ml) of the stock after each preceding amount has been almost absorbed, until all the stock is used. The entire process will take 17 or 18 minutes. It is very important to stir the rice constantly for even cooking and a creamy texture, although it will remain al dente.

6. When all the broth has been used, add the chicken, spinach, mushrooms, and cheese, stirring gently to mix. Cook for about 3 minutes, or until the flavors blend. Season with salt and pepper to taste.

7. Remove from the heat and add the brandy. Stir vigorously for 30 seconds to incorporate the brandy. Divide the risotto among 6 plates; garnish each with chopped parsley and a drizzle of extra-virgin olive oil.

SERVES 6

Note: Use leftover roasted chicken or roast a 1-pound (450-g) breast with the bone in. The breast will yield about ½ pound (230 g) of meat when pulled off the bone.

Fillet of Snapper with Tomatoes, Olives, and Roasted Potatoes

2 pounds (900 g) baking potatoes, peeled and cut into ⅓-inch (8-mm) slices
½ cup (120 ml) olive oil
Kosher salt and freshly ground black pepper to taste
Six 6-ounce (170 g) red snapper (rockfish) fillets, skin on
2 pounds (900 g) plum (egg) tomatoes, peeled, seeded, and chopped
*   (about 2 cups)*
¼ pound (115 g) kalamata olives, pitted and halved (about ¾ cup)
3 tablespoons chopped fresh flat-leaf parsley
1 tablespoon finely chopped lemon zest
1 cup (250 ml) dry white wine

1. Preheat the oven to 350°F (175°C).

2. In a large bowl, toss the potatoes with 2 tablespoons of the olive oil and season with salt and pepper. Spread in a roasting pan and bake for 35 to 40 minutes, until golden brown and cooked through. Using a metal spatula, gently loosen the potatoes from the pan and rearrange them so that they cover the pan in a single layer. Set aside.

3. Increase the oven temperature to 400°F (200°C).

4. Season the snapper with salt and pepper and arrange in a single layer over the potatoes.

5. In a bowl, gently toss the tomatoes with the olives, parsley, and lemon zest. Distribute this mixture evenly over the fillets and drizzle with the remaining 6 tablespoons (90 ml) of olive oil. Add the wine.

6. Bake for about 20 minutes, until the fillets flake when prodded with a fork. Lift the fillets from the pan and set aside. Carefully lift out the potatoes, leaving the tomato-olive mixture in the pan. Arrange the potatoes on 6 plates or a large serving platter and top with the fillets.

7. Set the roasting pan on a burner on top of the stove and heat the tomato-olive mixture over medium-high just until heated through. Spoon over the fillets and serve.

SERVES 6

While traveling in Portofino, we found a recipe similar to this one in every restaurant in this seaside town. There they serve it with whole fish—any fish that's fresh that day—but because our customers and American home cooks rarely like to bother with whole fish, we made our version with fillets. The snapper has a sturdy texture and good flavor that can stand up to the other ingredients. This is the perfect dish for early fall or during the summer when tomatoes are at their best.

(photograph on page 102)

Maybe they're not strictly Italian, but these lamb shanks are extremely popular in the restaurant. The bonus is that they are easy to make at home too. After you've seared the shanks, everything goes in a roasting pan and the whole dish cooks in the oven. It's delicious on the first day, but because it does not keep well, on the second day we cut the meat from the bones and mix it with onions, carrots, and some of the pan juices to make a pasta sauce.

Braised Lamb Shanks with Creamy Polenta

6 pounds (2.7 kg) lamb shanks (each about ¾ pound/340 g)
Salt and freshly ground black pepper
¼ cup (60 ml) olive oil
8 cups (1 kg) julienned red onions (about 4 large onions)
About 4 cups (140 g) loosely packed mint leaves (2 to 3 bunches)
2 cloves garlic, peeled
4 cups (1 l) Veal Stock (page 171) or canned low-sodium beef broth
4 cups (1 l) dry red wine
Creamy Polenta (recipe follows)

1. Preheat the oven to 350°F (175°C).

2. Liberally season the shanks with salt and pepper.

3. Divide the oil between 2 large sauté pans and heat over high heat until very hot. Add the shanks and brown, turning, for 20 to 30 minutes, until dark brown on all sides.

4. Spread the onions and mint leaves in a large roasting pan and nestle the garlic cloves in the onions. Put the shanks on top, pushing them into the vegetables. Pour the stock and wine into the pan, cover with aluminum foil, and bake for 2 hours. Remove the foil and bake for about 30 minutes longer, until the meat is tender.

5. Lift the shanks from the pan and set aside, covered, to keep warm. Strain the cooking liquid from the pan, discarding the onion-mint-garlic mixture. Simmer the liquid over medium-high heat for 5 to 6 minutes, until reduced to about 2 cups (500 ml) and slightly thickened. Season to taste with salt and pepper if necessary. Serve the shanks with the sauce spooned over them and the polenta alongside.

SERVES 6 TO 8

When customers ask for the recipe for this polenta, we tell them you can't go wrong with polenta if you mix it with cream, milk, and mascarpone cheese! We serve the polenta with Braised Lamb Shanks, but it is also an excellent side with short ribs, chicken, or pork. We've found that it goes well with sautéed shrimp but don't recommend serving it with fish, particularly delicate fillets. Its flavor might overpower the fish.

Creamy Polenta

2 cups (500 ml) milk
2 cups (500 ml) heavy (double) cream
¼ pound (115 g) stone-ground yellow cornmeal (maize flour)
   (about ¾ cup)
2 ounces (55 g) mascarpone cheese (about ¼ cup)
Salt to taste

1. In a large saucepan, bring the milk and cream to a boil over medium-high heat.

2. Slowly add the cornmeal to the hot milk mixture, whisking continuously to prevent lumps.

3. Reduce the heat to medium and simmer for 5 minutes, continuing to whisk to ensure the polenta is smooth.

4. Reduce the heat to very low and let the polenta simmer gently, uncovered, for 15 to 20 minutes, or until it is thick and creamy.

5. Stir in the mascarpone cheese, season with salt, and serve.

SERVES 6

Rosemary-Molasses Rack of Pork Roast

SOAKING LIQUID
1½ cups (375 ml) molasses
10 cloves garlic, peeled
1 tablespoon black peppercorns
2 cups (230 g) julienned onions
1 cup (15 g) broken fresh rosemary sprigs
2 teaspoons salt

PORK ROAST
One 5- to 5½-pound (2.25- to 2.5-kg) rack of pork (6 to 8 chops)
1 cup (115 g) coarsely chopped carrots
1 cup (115 g) coarsely chopped celery
1 cup (115 g) coarsely chopped onions
4 cloves garlic, peeled
4 sprigs fresh rosemary
2 tablespoons chopped fresh rosemary
Kosher salt and freshly ground black pepper to taste
1 cup (250 ml) dry white wine

1. To make the soaking liquid, in a pot large enough to hold the rack of pork, combine 2 quarts (2 l) of water with the molasses, garlic, peppercorns, onions, rosemary, and salt. Submerge the rack of pork, cover, and refrigerate for at least 24 hours.

2. Preheat the oven to 350°F (175°C).

3. In a large roasting pan, spread the carrots, celery, onions, garlic, and rosemary sprigs.

4. Remove the pork from the liquid and pat dry. Discard the liquid. Season the pork with the chopped rosemary, salt, and pepper. Lay the rack of pork on top of the vegetables in the roasting pan and pour 2 cups (500 ml) of water into the pan. Roast, uncovered, for 1½ to 2 hours, until a meat thermometer inserted into the thickest part of the meat registers 160°F (72°C) and the meat is deep brown.

5. Lift the pork from the roasting pan and set aside, covered, to keep warm. Add the wine to the pan and heat on top of the stove over high heat, stirring to scrape any vegetables sticking to the bottom of the pan.

6. Strain the liquid in the pan through a fine sieve into a saucepan, pushing against the vegetables to extract as much of the cooking juices as possible. There will be about 3 cups (750 ml). Defat the cooking juices and heat over medium-high heat until hot. Season with salt and pepper if necessary. Serve the sauce with the pork.

SERVES 6

Soaking the rack of pork in a rosemary-scented soaking liquid for 24 hours before roasting tenderizes and flavors the meat just enough for a delicious and succulent dish. Rack of pork is impressive without being overly fancy, in contrast to a crown roast. This is a nice, homey dish, especially when paired with Roasted-Garlic Mashed Potatoes (page 145) or Creamy Polenta (page 108).

We think this marinade goes especially well with venison, but it is also good with lamb or beef. Try it brushed on baby lamb chops or a paillard of chicken right before grilling to give them a flavor boost. You can make the marinade a day or two in advance, which in fact intensifies its flavor, but don't let the chops marinate too long or the marinade will overpower their natural flavor. For the best-tasting chops, grill them over a hot fire, although a hot broiler will caramelize the marinade too, which results in a nice, crispy crust.

Grilled Venison Chops with Balsamic Mustard Marinade

½ cup (20 g) loosely packed fresh basil leaves
¼ cup (55 g) Dijon mustard
¼ cup (60 ml) balsamic vinegar
½ cup (120 ml) olive oil
12 venison chops
Kosher salt and freshly ground black pepper to taste

1. To make the marinade, in a blender, combine the basil, mustard, and vinegar and puree until smooth. With the blender on low speed, drizzle the oil into the marinade until it is incorporated and the mixture has the consistency of thin mayonnaise.

2. Put the chops in a shallow glass or ceramic dish and pour half the marinade over them. Turn the chops and pour the remaining marinade over them. Cover and refrigerate for at least 20 minutes or up to 2 hours.

3. Prepare a charcoal or gas grill or preheat the broiler (griller).

4. Using a paper towel (kitchen paper), wipe the excess marinade from the chops and season them with salt and pepper. Grill for 3 to 4 minutes on each side, or until cooked to the desired degree of doneness. Cooking time will vary depending on the thickness of the chops.

SERVES 6

Note: Rib lamb chops can be substituted for venison chops in this recipe. If you do not wipe the marinade from the chops, the coals may flare up during grilling if the marinade drips onto them.

Venison Stew

2½ pounds (1.1 kg) venison stew meat, cut into large pieces
Salt and freshly ground black pepper to taste
½ cup (70 g) unbleached all-purpose (plain) flour
½ cup (120 ml) olive oil

½ pound (230 g) pancetta, finely diced (about 1⅓ cups)
2 cups (230 g) diced carrots (about 6 or 7)
2 cups (230 g) diced onions (about 3 or 4)
1½ cups (170 g) diced fennel (about 1 bulb)
3 large bay leaves
One 3-inch (7.5-cm) cinnamon stick
2 juniper berries, crushed with the flat side of a heavy knife blade or the
  back of a spoon
3 cups (750 ml) Veal Stock (page 171) or Chicken Stock (page 171)
3 cups (750 ml) dry red wine
4 cups (260 g) diced white cabbage (about ½ small head)
Chopped fresh flat-leaf parsley, for garnish

1. Season the venison with salt and pepper. Put the flour in a shallow dish and dredge the venison in it until well coated.

2. In a large sauté pan, heat ¼ cup (60 ml) of the olive oil over medium-high heat. Add venison pieces to cover the bottom of the pan in a single layer and sear for 2 to 3 minutes, until golden brown. Turn and sear the other side for 2 to 3 minutes. Transfer the seared meat to a platter and set aside. Repeat the process, cooking the meat in batches, until all is seared.

3. In a Dutch oven or other large pot, heat the remaining ¼ cup (60 ml) of oil over medium-low heat and sauté the pancetta, uncovered, for 20 to 25 minutes, until it is browned and the fat is rendered.

4. Drain all but 2 to 3 teaspoons of the fat from the pot and discard it. Add the carrots, onions, and fennel to the pancetta and cook for 5 minutes, stirring to coat the vegetables with the fat. Add the bay leaves, cinnamon stick, juniper berries, and meat, along with any collected juices. Add the stock and wine, raise the heat to medium-high, and bring to a simmer. Reduce the heat and simmer gently, uncovered, for 1½ hours. Season with salt and pepper.

5. Add the cabbage and cook for 30 minutes or longer, until the meat is tender. Sprinkle with parsley and serve.

SERVES 6

Note: You can substitute lamb for the venison in this stew.

When we traveled in northern Italy, we realized that two prevalent but subtle flavors in many hearty meat dishes were juniper berries and cinnamon. They provide a delicious accent to such strong-tasting meats as venison, lamb, and beef. Both are used in this rich, robust venison stew, which is wonderful on a chilly night with mashed potatoes or warm bread. Vincent has used leftover stew for individual pot pies made with a simple store-bought pastry crust—a very easy idea that works well with this recipe.

Leeks can be harvested well into autumn, and we like to take advantage of them while they are abundant. Their mild yet distinctive flavor goes nicely with the Italian sausage, garlic, and tomatoes in this savory tart, which is delicious as a light meal or as an appetizer with a glass of wine. The silken tart pastry can be made ahead of time and is easy to work with. The egg-cream mixture acts as a custard to bind the ingredients, making this tart similar to quiche but with more texture.

(photograph on page 82)

Sausage and Leek Tart with Fennel Crust

1 pound (450 g) leeks
¼ cup (60 ml) olive oil
¾ pound (340 g) sweet or mild Italian sausage, casings removed, coarsely crumbled
1 teaspoon chopped garlic
1 teaspoon kosher salt
3 large eggs
1 cup (250 ml) heavy (double) cream
2 tablespoons chopped fresh flat-leaf parsley
½ teaspoon freshly ground black pepper
Fennel Tart Dough (recipe follows)
4 cups (340 g) shredded fontina cheese (about ¾ pound)
12 plum tomatoes, cut into ¼-inch (6-mm) slices, drained on paper towels (about 2 pounds/900 g)

1. Prepare the leeks by trimming off the green stems and slicing the white parts in half lengthwise, then cutting crosswise to make ½-inch-wide (1.3-cm) half-moon shapes. Transfer to a bowl of cold water and let stand for about 5 minutes. During this time, any sand in the leeks will sink to the bottom of the bowl. Scoop the leeks from the bowl and drain.

2. In a sauté pan, heat 2 tablespoons of the oil and cook the sausage over medium heat for 7 to 8 minutes, until the fat is rendered and the meat browns lightly. Using a spoon, break up the meat as it cooks. Drain and set aside. Discard the fat.

3. In another pan, heat the remaining 2 tablespoons of oil and cook the leeks and garlic over medium-low heat for about 15 minutes, until the leeks are very soft but not browned. Sprinkle with ½ teaspoon of the salt during cooking. Remove from the pan and set aside to cool.

4. In a bowl, combine the eggs, cream, parsley, remaining ½ teaspoon of salt, and the pepper. Whisk until smooth.

5. On a lightly floured surface, using a lightly floured rolling pin, roll the

dough (pastry) until about 12 inches (30.5 cm) in diameter (large enough to fit into a 10-inch/25-cm tart pan). Fold the dough in half and then in half again to make a triangular package. Position the pointed tip in the center of the tart pan and unfold the dough to fill the pan. Press the dough against the sides of the pan and over the bottom. Trim off the overhanging dough. Refrigerate the tart pan for 20 minutes.

6. Preheat the oven to 350°F (175°C).

7. Arrange the leeks in a single layer in the tart pan. Spread the sausage meat over the leeks and then top evenly with cheese. Arrange the tomato slices in a spiral pattern over the cheese to cover completely. Carefully and slowly pour the egg-cream mixture over the tomatoes so that it soaks into the tart and does not overflow the pan. Set the pan on a baking sheet and bake for 50 to 60 minutes, until the custard is set and the edges of the dough are golden. Let the tart cool in the pan before removing and cutting into wedges.

SERVES 6

Fennel Tart Dough

2¼ cups (315 g) unbleached all-purpose (plain) flour
1 cup (2 sticks/230 g) unsalted butter, cut into cubes and chilled
1 tablespoon crushed fennel seeds
1 teaspoon kosher salt
1 large egg, lightly beaten

1. In a food processor fitted with the metal blade, combine the flour, butter, fennel seeds, and salt. Pulse 9 or 10 times, until the mixture resembles coarse crumbs. Do not overmix.

2. In a small bowl, whisk together 2 tablespoons water and egg. With the food processor running, add the egg mixture through the feeding tube. Pulse 8 to 10 times, just until the dough comes together in a cohesive mass. Do not overmix or the dough will be tough.

(continued on page 114)   AUTUMN ■ 113

Fennel Tart Dough
(continued from page 113)

3. Remove the dough from the food processor and form into a ball. Flatten into a disc about 6 inches (15 cm) wide and 1½ inches (4 cm) thick, wrap in plastic, and refrigerate for at least 1 hour before using. Let the dough stand at room temperature for about 15 minutes before rolling out and using in a recipe.

MAKES ENOUGH FOR ONE 10- TO 11-INCH (25- TO 28-CM) TART

Note: The dough can be made 2 days in advance and refrigerated. When making this dough, work at a steady pace. Measure all ingredients before beginning and make sure the butter is well chilled. The large amount of butter softens quickly, which can make the dough difficult to handle. This is particularly true in humid or very warm weather.

Ducks Stuffed with Prunes and Roasted Garlic

> When we decided to develop a duck dish for the restaurant, we came up with this very simple presentation. The prunes and roasted garlic stuffed into the ducks permeate the meat during roasting from the inside out. The prunes are delicious as a side dish with the ducks and take the place of the fancy sweet fruit sauce that is so often served.

½ pound (230 g) pitted dried prunes
4 large heads Roasted Garlic (page 168; about 1 cup)
Grated zest of 1 lemon
1 teaspoon salt, plus more to taste, and ½ teaspoon freshly ground black pepper, plus more to taste
Two 3- to 4-pound (1.4- to 1.8-kg) ducks
1 large carrot, coarsely chopped
1 medium onion, coarsely chopped
1 large sprig fresh rosemary
1 cup (250 ml) Duck Stock (page 172) or Chicken Stock (page 171)
1 tablespoon flour

1. Preheat the oven to 350°F (175°C).

2. Soak the prunes in warm water to cover for about 10 minutes, or until plump. Drain, discarding the liquid.

3. Squeeze the roasted garlic cloves from their skins. In a medium bowl, mix the garlic with the prunes, lemon zest, 1 teaspoon salt, and ½ teaspoon pepper.

4. Wash the ducks and discard the giblets or reserve for another use. Trim excess fat from the ducks if necessary.

5. Stuff the cavities of the ducks with the prune and garlic mixture. Close the cavities, either by sewing loosely with cotton kitchen twine or by fastening with toothpicks. If you wish, tie the legs together with twine. Sprinkle the ducks with salt and pepper to taste.

6. In a large roasting pan, spread out the chopped carrot and onion. Add the rosemary and 1 cup (250 ml) water and place the ducks on top of the vegetables. Roast, uncovered, for about 2½ hours, or until the skin is crisp and golden and a meat thermometer inserted in the thickest part of the thigh meat registers 180° to 185°F (82° to 85°C). (After 1 hour, add as much as 1 cup/250 ml water, if necessary, to preserve the pan juices.)

7. Reduce the oven temperature to 200°F (95°C). Transfer the ducks to a serving platter, cover loosely with foil, and place in the warm oven.

8. Place the roasting pan on the stove, add the stock, and cook over medium heat for 2 to 3 minutes, scraping any browned bits from the bottom of the pan.

9. Strain the contents of the pan into a small saucepan and let stand for about 5 minutes. Skim the fat from the surface.

10. In a small bowl, whisk the flour into ½ cup (120 ml) cold water and then add to the sauce. Bring to a boil and cook, whisking constantly, for 4 to 5 minutes. Season with salt and pepper to taste.

11. To serve, remove the stuffing from the ducks and set aside. Cut off the wings and legs and slice the breast meat. Garnish each serving with stuffing and drizzle with sauce.

SERVES 6

Pumpkin Cheesecake

GRAHAM CRACKER CRUST
1¼ cups (175 g) graham cracker (wheatmeal) crumbs
3 tablespoons (45 g) unsalted butter, melted
1 tablespoon sugar

FILLING
1 pound (450 g) mascarpone cheese (2 cups)
1 pound (450 g) dry ricotta cheese (2 cups; see Note)
½ cup (100 g) sugar (see Note)
Pinch of salt
3 large eggs
¼ teaspoon ground ginger
1 teaspoon ground cinnamon
2 cups (450 g) Fresh Pumpkin Puree (recipe follows) or unsweetened canned pumpkin puree

1. To prepare the graham cracker crust, in a medium bowl, combine the graham cracker crumbs, butter, and sugar and mix with a fork or your fingertips until the crumbs absorb the butter and hold together.

2. Wrap the outside of a 10-inch (25-cm) springform pan with a large sheet of heavy-duty aluminum foil to come about halfway up the sides of the pan.

3. Press the graham cracker mixture into the bottom of the pan in an even layer.

4. Preheat the oven to 375°F (175°C).

5. To make the filling, in an electric mixer on medium speed, mix the mascarpone, ricotta, sugar, and salt for about 1 minute, until well mixed. Scrape the bowl of the mixer and mix for another minute.

6. Add the eggs, one at a time, beating for about 30 seconds after each addition until each egg is incorporated. Add the ginger and cinnamon, scrape the bowl, and mix for 30 seconds. Add the pumpkin puree and mix for another 30 seconds.

(continued on page 118)

Pumpkin Cheesecake
(continued from page 116)

7. Scrape the filling into the prepared springform pan. Set the pan in a larger roasting pan and place on the center rack of the oven. Add enough hot water to come halfway up the foil wrapped around the pan. Bake for 50 minutes to 1 hour, or until the blade of a knife inserted into the cake comes out clean.

8. Remove from the oven and refrigerate immediately. Chill for at least 4 hours. To serve, remove foil and release the sides of the springform pan.

SERVES 12 TO 16; MAKES ONE 10-INCH (25-CM) CHEESECAKE

Note: Dry ricotta cheese can be bought in some Italian markets. If you cannot purchase it, make your own: line a colander with cheesecloth and put about 1 1/2 pounds (675 g) of ricotta in the colander. Set the colander over a bowl to catch the draining liquid. Cover and refrigerate for at least 4 hours and for up to 8 hours. The longer the cheese drains, the drier it will be.

If you use canned puree, increase the amount of sugar to 1 1/4 cups (260 g).

Fresh Pumpkin Puree

1 very large sugar pumpkin (about 10 pounds/4.5 kg) or 2 or 3 small
   sugar pumpkins (3 to 5 pounds/1.4 to 2.2 kg each)
2 cups (400 g)sugar

1. Preheat the oven to 350°F (175°C).

2. Cut the pumpkin (or pumpkins) in half, remove the seeds, and place the halves, cut sides down, on a baking sheet. Pierce the skins with a fork.

3. Bake for about 1½ to 2 hours, or until the flesh is very soft.

4. Let cool to room temperature.

5. When cool enough to handle, separate the flesh from the skins. You should have at least 6 cups of pumpkin flesh.

6. In a large, heavy-bottomed saucepan, cook the sugar over medium-high heat until it caramelizes and turns a rich amber color. Add the pumpkin, being careful not to splatter the hot caramel.

7. Reduce the heat to medium and simmer, uncovered, for about 1 hour, stirring often, until the sugar melts and incorporates with the pumpkin.

8. Remove from heat and cool to room temperature. Use immediately or cover and refrigerate.

MAKES ABOUT 6 CUPS

Note: The puree can be frozen for up to a month. For easy use, freeze it in heavy-duty self-sealing plastic bags in 2-cup amounts.

Fresco's Biscotti

5 cups (700 g) all-purpose (plain) flour
1⅛ teaspoons baking powder
Pinch of salt
3 large eggs, separated
1¼ cups (260 g) sugar
½ cup (1 stick/115 g) unsalted butter, melted and cooled to
*   room temperature*
¼ teaspoon pure vanilla extract

1. Preheat the oven to 350°F (175°C). Line a baking sheet with parchment paper and set aside.

2. In a large bowl, whisk together the flour, baking powder, and salt. Set aside.

3. In the bowl of an electric mixer, combine the egg yolks and half (½ cup plus 2 tablespoons) of the sugar. With the mixer set on medium-high, beat until the sugar dissolves and the mixture is pale yellow.

4. In a clean, dry bowl and using clean, dry beaters, whip the egg whites until soft peaks form. With the mixer running, add the remaining sugar a little at a time, until all the sugar is incorporated and the peaks are stiff. Using a rubber spatula, gently fold the whites into the yolk mixture. There will be a few specks of the whites showing. Add the butter and vanilla and fold just until mixed.

5. With the mixer set on medium, mix about ¼ cup of the dry ingredients into the batter. Continue adding the dry ingredients, ¼ cup at a time, until all is incorporated. The dough will be very stiff at the end of mixing, and you will have to use a wooden spoon to mix in the last of the dry ingredients.

6. Turn the dough out onto a lightly floured surface and divide into 2 long, slightly flattened (not round) logs, each 2½ to 3 inches (6.5 to 7.5 cm) wide and about 1½ inches (3.8 cm) high. With a dull knife, make a shallow indentation down the center of the logs. (This will prevent cracking.) Transfer the

logs to the baking sheet, leaving an inch or two (2.5 to 5 cm) between them, and press them gently to flatten the bottoms slightly. (You may find it easier to use 2 baking sheets.) Bake for 20 minutes, until set and firm. Remove from the oven and cool on wire racks for 20 minutes. Do not turn off the oven and do not discard the parchment paper on the baking sheet.

7. Using a serrated knife, cut the logs diagonally into ½-inch (1.3-cm) slices that are about 3 inches (7.5 cm) long. Lay the cookies on the baking sheet and bake about 10 minutes longer, until they are lightly browned and the edges are crisp. Cool on wire racks. (You may have to do this in batches, depending on the number and size of your baking sheets.) Serve immediately or store in an airtight container for up to 2 months.

MAKES ABOUT 50 COOKIES

Note: The recipe can easily be doubled. When making the following variations, leave the nuts whole, so that when the logs are sliced, the nuts will also be sliced into attractive shapes and sizes.

Variations

Fresco's Cinnamon-Almond Biscotti
Add 10 ounces (280 g) of toasted whole almonds and 1 tablespoon of ground cinnamon to the dough in step 4 when you add the butter and vanilla. Proceed with the recipe as written.

Fresco's Hazelnut-Raisin Biscotti
Add 6 ounces (170 g) of toasted whole hazelnuts, 6 ounces (170 g) of golden raisins (sultanas), and 2 teaspoons of fennel seeds to the dough in step 4 when you add the butter and vanilla. Proceed with the recipe as written.

Fresco's Walnut-Chocolate Biscotti
Add 6 ounces (170 g) of toasted whole walnuts and 8 ounces (230 g) of chopped semisweet (bitter) chocolate to the dough in step 4 when you add the butter and vanilla. Proceed with the recipe as written.

sandwiches

Sandwiches are popular at lunchtime, and we offer big, full-flavored ones made with our own fragrant Tuscan Bread (page 173). Many Italian markets, bakeries, and even restaurants sell a similar peasant-style bread, so if you don't want to bake your own, you most likely can buy a delicious freshly baked loaf that is very similar. Because we have grills going nearly all the time, we grill the bread, but you can toast or broil it instead. Depending on the season, we change the sandwich fillings. Some of our favorites include: a rare grilled tuna steak between grilled bread as a very unexpected "tuna" sandwich; a sandwich with grilled portobello mushrooms, which have the texture of steak, with cheese melted over the top; a Veal Milanese sandwich; an open-faced grilled steak sandwich; and a grilled chicken and pepperonata sandwich.

Grilled Portobello Mushroom Sandwich

1 large red onion, thinly sliced
2 tablespoons red wine vinegar
1 teaspoon sugar
6 large portobello mushrooms, stemmed (about 1 pound/450 g)
3 tablespoons olive oil
Kosher salt and freshly ground black pepper to taste
12 slices Tuscan Bread (page 173) or other peasant-style bread
½ pound (230 g) fontina cheese, thinly sliced
1 cup Rosemary Mayonnaise (page 168)
3 large tomatoes, cut into 12 slices
2 cups (85 g) arugula (rocket) leaves

1. In a small glass or ceramic bowl, combine the onions with the vinegar and sugar, mix gently, and set aside to marinate for about 30 minutes.

2. Prepare a charcoal or gas grill and preheat the broiler (griller).

3. Brush the mushroom caps on both sides with olive oil and season with salt and pepper. Grill for about 3 minutes on each side, until browned. Remove from the grill and set aside. Grill the bread on both sides until lightly toasted.

4. Slice the mushrooms vertically almost all the way through (see Note), leaving them attached on one side so that they can be fanned or spread out to cover a slice of bread. Top each mushroom with sliced cheese. Lay the mushroom caps on a baking sheet and broil for 1 to 2 minutes, just until the cheese melts.

5. Spread the mayonnaise on one side of each slice of toast. Set a mushroom cap on 6 of the slices and top the mushrooms with onions, 2 slices of tomatoes, and arugula. Top with the remaining slices of toast. Cut in half and serve immediately.

SERVES 6

Note: *It's important to keep the mushrooms intact at their base so that they do not separate during broiling; this prevents the cheese from dripping through. You may toast the bread in a toaster or the broiler if you prefer.*

Open-Faced Grilled Steak Sandwich

(photograph on page 125)

3½ ounces (100 g) sirloin strip steak
Kosher salt and freshly ground black pepper
   to taste
3 tablespoons (45 g) unsalted butter
1 teaspoon finely chopped garlic
6 slices Tuscan Bread (page 173) or other
   peasant-style bread
½ recipe Roasted-Garlic Mashed Potatoes
   (page 145)

1. Prepare a charcoal or gas grill or preheat the broiler (griller).

2. Season the steak with salt and pepper and grill for 2 to 3 minutes on each side, or until the meat reaches the desired degree of doneness. Slice the steak diagonally into 12 slices.

3. In a small saucepan, heat the butter and garlic over medium-low heat just until melted. Do not let the garlic burn. Brush both sides of the bread with the garlic but-ter. Grill the bread for 1 to 2 minutes on each side, until lightly browned.

4. Spread the mashed potatoes over each slice of bread and top with steak. Serve immediately.

SERVES 6

Note: *Vincent recommends serving this with a green or tomato salad.*

Veal Milanese Sandwich

(photograph on page 125)

12 slices Tuscan Bread (page 173) or other
   peasant-style bread
6 Milanese Veal cutlets (½ recipe, page 149)
½ pound (230 g) pepper or plain pecorino cheese
   or Parmesan cheese, thinly sliced (see Note)
1 cup (250 ml) Rosemary Mayonnaise (page 168)
3 large tomatoes, cut into 12 slices
2 cups (85 g) arugula (rocket) leaves

1. Preheat the broiler (griller). Spray a baking sheet lightly with olive oil spray.

2. Toast the bread under the broiler, turning once, until lightly browned. Set aside.

3. Lay the veal cutlets on a baking sheet and top each with cheese. Broil for 2 to 3 minutes, until the cheese melts.

4. Spread the mayonnaise on one side of each slice of toast and top 6 of the slices with the veal and cheese. Lay 2 tomato slices on each piece of veal and top each evenly with arugula. Place the remaining slices of toast on top, cut in half, and serve immediately.

SERVES 6

Grilled Chicken and Pepperonata Sandwich

Six 4- to 5-ounce (115- to 140-g) boneless,
   skinless chicken breasts
2 tablespoons Fresco Seasoning (page 170)
2 tablespoons olive oil
1 teaspoon minced garlic
2 large red bell peppers (capsicums), seeded and
   thinly sliced
1 large onion, thinly sliced
Kosher salt and freshly ground black pepper
   to taste
12 slices Tuscan Bread (page 173) or other
   peasant-style bread
½ pound (230 g) fontina cheese, cut into 12 slices
3 beefsteak tomatoes, cut into 12 slices
2 cups (85 g) arugula (rocket) leaves

1. Prepare a charcoal or gas grill or preheat the broiler (griller).

2. Season the chicken with the seasoning mix and grill for 3 to 5 minutes on each side, until cooked through. Set aside.

3. In a large sauté pan, heat the olive oil over medium heat. Cook the garlic for about 30 seconds, until golden. Add the peppers and onions and cook for 15 to 20 minutes, until softened and the onions start to caramelize. Season to taste with salt and pepper and set aside.

4. Grill the bread for 1 to 2 minutes on each side, until lightly browned. Top 6 slices with chicken, then spoon an even amount of the peppers and onions on each chicken breast and top with cheese slices. Broil just until the cheese melts.

5. Arrange 2 slices of tomato and some arugula on each sandwich and top with the remaining slices of toast. Cut in half and serve immediately.

SERVES 6

Grilled Tuna Sandwich

12 thin slices pancetta
1½ pounds (675 g) tuna loin, cut into 6 thick pieces
Kosher salt and freshly ground black pepper to taste
12 slices Tuscan Bread (page 173) or other
   peasant-style bread
1 cup Rosemary Mayonnaise (page 168)
3 large tomatoes, cut into 12 slices
2 cups (85 g) arugula (rocket) leaves

1. Preheat the oven to 350°F (175°C). Prepare a charcoal or gas grill or preheat the broiler (griller). Brush the grill rack with a little olive oil to prevent sticking.

2. Lay the pancetta on a baking sheet and bake for 8 to 10 minutes, until browned and crispy. Transfer the pancetta to paper towels (kitchen paper) to drain.

3. Season the tuna pieces with salt and pepper and grill for 2 minutes on each side for medium-rare tuna. Grill the slices of bread on both sides until lightly browned.

4. Spread the mayonnaise on one side of each slice of toast. Arrange the tuna on 6 slices of the toast and top each with 2 slices of pancetta, 2 slices of tomatoes, and arugula. Top with the remaining slices of toast. Cut in half and serve immediately.

SERVES 6

Left to right: Veal Milanese Sandwich, Open-Faced Grilled Steak Sandwich (both recipes on page 123)

WINTER

White beans and cabbage are a great flavor combination, one that fits our definition of soup to a tee: nothing fancy but instead hearty and comforting, especially important in the wintertime. Serve this soup as a first course or as a light meal with a green salad and loaf of bread.

White Bean and Cabbage Soup

2 tablespoons olive oil
6 ounces (170 g) pancetta, finely diced
2 cups (230 g) coarsely chopped onions
1½ tablespoons chopped garlic
1 tablespoon chopped fresh rosemary leaves
1 tablespoon chopped fresh flat-leaf parsley
1 tablespoon chopped fresh oregano
½ teaspoon crushed red pepper flakes, or to taste
1 cup (230 g) crushed canned tomatoes
½ pound (230 g) dried cannellini (white kidney beans), rinsed and
    picked over
4 cups (1 l) Chicken Stock (page 171)
Kosher salt to taste
4 cups (340 g) coarsely chopped cabbage (about one ¾-pound head)
Extra-virgin olive oil, for drizzling

1. In a large stockpot, heat the oil over low heat and cook the pancetta, uncovered, for 15 to 20 minutes, until it is browned and the fat is rendered.

2. Add the onions, garlic, rosemary, parsley, oregano, and red pepper flakes and cook for 10 to 15 minutes, until the onions soften.

3. Add the tomatoes, beans, stock, and 4 cups (1 l) water and bring to a boil. Reduce the heat to a simmer and cook, partially covered, for 1 hour. Season to taste with salt, add the cabbage, and cook for 30 minutes to 1 hour longer, or until the cabbage is softened and the beans are very tender. Add more salt if necessary.

4. Ladle the soup into bowls and drizzle each serving with olive oil.

SERVES 6

Note: The soup keeps in the refrigerator for up to 2 days in a covered container. It keeps in the freezer for up to 2 months.

Pages 126–27, left to right:
Cranberry Apple Tart with Hazelnut
Crust (recipe on page 158),
Panettone Bread Pudding
(recipe on page 160)

Lentil Soup with Sausage and Escarole

3 tablespoons (45 ml) olive oil
6 ounces (170 g) sweet or mild Italian sausage, casings removed
    and coarsely chopped
1 cup (115 g) finely diced carrots
1 cup (115 g) finely diced onions
1 cup (115 g) finely diced fennel (about 1 small bulb)
2 tablespoons chopped garlic
1 tablespoon crushed red pepper flakes
10½ ounces (295 g) dried brown lentils
2 quarts (2 l) Chicken Stock (page 171)
10½ ounces (295 g) escarole (chicory), washed and chopped
    (about 6 cups)
5 tablespoons (37 g) freshly grated Parmesan cheese
Salt to taste
Finely chopped fresh flat-leaf parsley, for garnish

1. In a large stockpot, heat the oil over medium-high heat. Add the sausage, carrots, onions, fennel, garlic, and red pepper flakes and cook, covered, for about 12 minutes, until the sausage begins to brown and render its fat.

2. Add the lentils and stock and bring to a boil. Reduce the heat to medium and simmer, uncovered, for 20 minutes. Add the escarole and cook for about 25 minutes, or until the lentils are very soft. Stir in the cheese and season to taste with salt. Ladle the soup into bowls and garnish with parsley.

SERVES 6

Note: To make plain lentil soup, omit the sausage and escarole. After adding the lentils and stock, cook the soup for 45 minutes, or until the lentils are very soft. Transfer 1 cup (250 ml) of the vegetables to a food processor and process until smooth. Return to the soup, stir, and proceed with the recipe.

Lentils are traditionally eaten in Italy on New Year's Day because they signify health, wealth, and happiness. This is a straightforward lentil soup with sausage and escarole added, both of which may be omitted when you want plain lentil soup (see Note). We serve it on New Year's Eve, partly because of tradition and partly because it's Marion's good luck soup—so how could we begin a new year without it?

Black Bean Soup with Lemon Oil and Garlic Croutons

SOUP

½ pound (230 g) dried black beans, rinsed and picked over
¾ cup (85 g) finely diced carrots
¾ cup (85 g) finely diced onions
¾ cup (85 g) finely diced fennel (1 small bulb)
One 2-ounce (55-g) piece prosciutto
½ to 1 teaspoon crushed red pepper flakes, or to taste
1 tablespoon chopped garlic
1 teaspoon kosher salt, or to taste

LEMON OIL

3 tablespoons (45 ml) extra-virgin olive oil
1½ tablespoons fresh lemon juice

Garlic Croutons (recipe follows)

1. To make the soup, in a large stockpot, combine 6 cups (1.5 l) water with the beans, carrots, onions, fennel, prosciutto, red pepper flakes, garlic, and salt and bring to a boil over high heat. Reduce the heat to medium-high or medium and simmer, uncovered, for about 1 hour 15 minutes, or until the beans are very tender.

2. Remove the prosciutto and discard. Transfer 1½ cups (375 ml) of the soup to a food processor and puree until smooth. Return the puree to the pot and season the soup with more salt if needed.

3. To make the lemon oil, in a small bowl, whisk the oil and lemon juice until blended.

4. Ladle the soup into serving bowls, drizzle with lemon oil, and garnish with Garlic Croutons before serving.

SERVES 6

Garlic Croutons

3 large slices Tuscan Bread (page 173) or other peasant-style bread
1 whole clove garlic
2 tablespoons extra-virgin olive oil

1. Toast the bread until lightly browned.

2. Holding the garlic between your thumb and forefinger, rub it on both sides of the bread slices.

3. Drizzle the bread with the oil and cut into ½-inch (1.3-cm) croutons. Serve warm.

MAKES ABOUT 3 CUPS CROUTONS

Note: Because these croutons are best served warm, make them just before serving the soup.

Cavatelli with Sausage Ragù and Broccoli Rabe

1 pound (450 g) mild Italian sausage
½ pound (230 g) broccoli rabe (about 1 bunch)
1 medium onion, coarsely chopped
1 large carrot, coarsely chopped
1 small bulb fennel, trimmed and coarsely chopped
½ cup (120 ml) olive oil
1 teaspoon crushed red pepper flakes
3 large cloves garlic, finely chopped (about 2 tablespoons)
1 cup (250 ml) tomato puree
1 cup (250 ml) dry Italian red wine
1 cup (250 ml) Chicken Stock (page 171)
Salt and freshly ground black pepper to taste
1 pound (450 g) dried cavatelli or small shell-shaped pasta
Freshly grated Parmesan cheese, for garnish

We especially like ragùs, which cook for a long time to let the flavors deepen and mellow. In this recipe, instead of big chunks of sausage mixed into the pasta, the sausage is part of the ragù sauce, which makes its flavor wonderfully intense. The broccoli rabe is added at the end of the recipe because, if added any sooner, it tends to overpower the other ingredients, and all you taste is broccoli rabe.

(continued on page 132)

1. In a deep skillet of briskly simmering water, blanch the sausage for 5 minutes. Lift from the water and set aside to cool. When cool, remove the sausage from its casings and crumble the meat. (You will have about 3 cups.)

2. In a saucepan of boiling water, blanch the broccoli rabe for about 4 minutes, until barely tender. Drain and cool. When cool, coarsely chop. (You will have about 2 cups.)

3. In a food processor fitted with the metal blade, process the onion until finely ground. Set aside. Process the carrot until finely ground. Set aside. Process the fennel until finely ground. (You will have about 1 cup of each vegetable.)

4. In a large saucepan or large, deep skillet, heat the olive oil over low heat. Add the onion, carrot, fennel, red pepper flakes, and garlic and cook for about 30 minutes, or until the moisture evaporates.

5. Add the sausage, tomato puree, wine, and stock. Stir to mix and simmer over medium-low heat, stirring occasionally, for 1½ hours, or until the sauce thickens and is reduced by three-quarters. Season to taste with salt and pepper.

6. Meanwhile, bring a large pot of lightly salted water to a boil and cook the pasta for 6 to 8 minutes, until barely al dente. Drain and add the pasta to the sauce.

7. Add the broccoli rabe and cook, stirring gently, for 2 to 3 minutes, until heated through. Transfer to a serving platter and garnish with Parmesan cheese.

SERVES 6

Ravioli with Sausage and Spinach

2 tablespoons olive oil
½ pound (230 g) fresh spinach leaves
½ pound (230 g) sweet or mild Italian sausage, crumbled
1½ cups (215 g) finely diced fresh mozzarella cheese
1½ cups (155 g) freshly grated Parmesan cheese
¾ cup (170 g) fresh ricotta cheese
¼ cup (10 g) finely chopped fresh flat-leaf parsley
Kosher salt and freshly ground black pepper to taste

5 large eggs (see Note)
Sixty 2½-inch (6.4-cm) fresh pasta squares or wonton wrappers
(about 1 pound/450 g; see Note)
3 cups (750 ml) Basic Tomato Sauce (page 169)

1. In a large skillet, heat the oil over medium-high heat and sauté the spinach for 2 to 3 minutes, tossing until completely wilted. Transfer to a plate to cool. Divide the spinach into thirds and, using your hands or a kitchen towel, squeeze the moisture from the spinach. Chop finely and transfer to a bowl.

2. Add the sausage, mozzarella, Parmesan, ricotta, 2 tablespoons of the parsley, and salt and pepper to taste. Stir in 2 of the eggs until well mixed.

3. In a small bowl, make an egg wash by whisking together the remaining 3 eggs and 3 tablespoons of water.

4. On a work surface, lay a pasta square or wonton wrapper and spoon 1 generous tablespoon (about 1 ounce/30 g) of filling onto the center. Using your fingertips or a brush, dampen the edges of the pasta with the egg wash and lay a second square on top. Press the edges together, using your fingertips or a fork to crimp the edges of the ravioli closed, pressing out any trapped air in the process, and making sure to form a tight seal. If necessary, dab a little more egg wash on the pasta to ensure a tight seal. Set aside on a baking sheet or tray and cover with a damp, well-wrung kitchen towel. Continue with the remaining filling and pasta to make 30 ravioli. Arrange the ravioli in a single layer on the baking sheet so that they do not stick together.

5. Bring a large pot of lightly salted water to a boil and, using a slotted spoon or spatula, submerge 5 or 6 ravioli in the water and cook for about 5 minutes, until al dente. Using a slotted spoon, lift the ravioli from the water, let drain, and set on a warm serving platter. Hold the platter in a warm (200°F/95°C) oven while cooking all the ravioli. Let the water return to a boil between batches. When all the ravioli are cooked, reserve ½ cup (120 ml) of the pasta cooking water.

6. In a large saucepan, heat the tomato sauce over medium heat. Add the reserved cooking water and simmer for 2 minutes. Spoon the sauce over the ravioli on the serving platter, taking care to cover all the ravioli. Sprinkle with the remaining 2 tablespoons of parsley and serve immediately.

SERVES 6

(continued on page 134)

Marion and Vincent are partial to sausage, so it turns up frequently in our recipes. We particularly like it mixed with spinach and cheese as a filling for ravioli, served with a simple tomato sauce. You can use frozen spinach instead of fresh, but be sure to squeeze all the excess moisture from it.

Ravioli with Sausage
and Spinach
(continued from page 133)

Note: Fresh pasta sheets are often sold in specialty stores or Italian markets. Wonton wrappers, which are an acceptable substitute, are readily available in supermarkets. If using wonton wrappers, you will not need to use the egg wash; moisten the edges of the wrappers with plain water.

To freeze, lay the uncooked ravioli on a baking sheet lined with parchment paper and sprinkle them with about 1 cup (140 g) of semolina flour. Cover with plastic wrap and freeze for 2 to 3 days. Do not freeze any longer or the ravioli will dry out and crack when cooked in boiling water. The ravioli can be boiled still frozen; no need to thaw first.

Mom's Meatballs

Although these meatballs are integral to Mom's Lasagne (page 135), they can stand alone as a meal, either spooned over pasta or not. Like many of our others, this recipe reflects our Brooklyn as well as our Italian roots—and the two are so intertwined it's sometimes hard to tell where they part. The meatballs are a version of those that Marion made for her family and the meatballs Vincent has always made. They are browned before they are cooked in the tomato sauce, which removes a little fat and gives them a firmer texture.

MEATBALLS
*One 3-ounce (85-g) piece Tuscan Bread (page 173) or other
   peasant-style bread
¾ pound (340 g) ground (minced) beef
1 large egg, lightly beaten
2 tablespoons chopped fresh flat-leaf parsley
3 cloves garlic, chopped
½ cup (55 g) freshly grated Parmesan cheese
1 teaspoon kosher salt
1½ cups (375 ml) olive oil*

SAUCE
*¼ cup (60 ml) olive oil
3 cloves garlic, chopped
3 cups (750 ml) tomato puree
2 tablespoons chopped fresh basil
1 tablespoon chopped fresh flat-leaf parsley
¼ teaspoon crushed red pepper flakes
Kosher salt to taste*

1. To make the meatballs, in a small bowl, pour 2 tablespoons hot water over the bread and let stand for about 10 minutes.

2. In a large bowl, combine the beef, egg, parsley, garlic, cheese, and salt and, using your hands or a wooden spoon, mix well.

3. Squeeze any excess water from the bread and tear the bread into small pieces. Add to the meat mixture and mix again. Divide the mixture into 6 equal portions and roll each one into a ball about 2 inches (5 cm) in diameter.

4. In a large skillet, heat the olive oil over medium-high heat and cook the meatballs, turning so that they brown on all sides, for about 15 minutes, until golden brown. Drain on paper towels (kitchen paper).

5. To make the sauce, in a saucepan, heat the olive oil over medium-low heat and sauté the garlic for 3 to 4 minutes, until lightly browned. Add the tomato purée, basil, parsley, and red pepper flakes and cook until simmering. Season to taste with salt.

6. Add the meatballs to the sauce and cook, covered, for about 30 minutes, until cooked through. Remove from the heat and let the meatballs cool in the sauce.

SERVES 6; MAKES 6 MEATBALLS AND 2½ CUPS (630 ML) SAUCE

Mom's Lasagne

¾ pound (340 g) sweet or mild Italian sausage
3 cups (300 g) freshly grated Parmesan cheese (about 11 ounces)
2 cups (280 g) diced fresh mozzarella cheese
1 cup (230 g) fresh ricotta cheese
2 large eggs, lightly beaten
½ cup (20 g) chopped fresh flat-leaf parsley
Salt and freshly ground black pepper to taste
1 recipe Mom's Meatballs (page 134)
2½ cups (630 ml) tomato purée
1 pound (450 g) fresh pasta sheets or 8 ounces (230 g) dried
   lasagne sheets

1. In a large saucepan, combine the sausage with enough cold water to cover by 1 inch (2.5 cm), bring to a simmer over medium-high heat, and cook for about 10 minutes. Transfer to a bowl filled with cold water to stop the cooking. Remove the casings and crumble or chop the meat coarsely. Cover and refrigerate.

Nearly every Italian American makes a lasagne similar to this one. It always includes Italian sausage, a cheese mixture of ricotta, mozzarella, and Parmesan, and meatballs. This is often a holiday dish, simply because making it is a laborious process and requires the time we tend to devote to special meals. But the effort is well worth it!

(continued on page 136)

2. In a bowl, combine 2 cups (200 g) of the Parmesan, the mozzarella, ricotta, eggs, and parsley and season to taste with salt and pepper.

3. Lift the meatballs from their sauce and crumble them. Cover and refrigerate.

4. Combine the sauce from the meatballs with the tomato puree. If the mixture does not measure 5 cups (1.2 l), add more puree to make 5 cups.

5. If using dried lasagne, bring a large pot of lightly salted water to a boil and cook the pasta for 8 to 10 minutes, until barely al dente. Drain and separate the sheets to cool. If using fresh pasta, do not cook it before assembling the lasagne.

6. Preheat the oven to 350°F (175°C).

7. In a 9 × 13-inch (23 × 33-cm) baking pan that is at least 2 inches (5 cm) deep, spread 1 cup (250 ml) of the tomato sauce over the bottom, tilting the pan if necessary to spread evenly. Lay a quarter of the lasagne sheets over the sauce, overlapping slightly and trimming if necessary to fit.

8. Spread a third of the cheese mixture evenly over the pasta. Top with a third of the sausage and then a third of the meatballs. Spoon 1 cup (250 ml) of the sauce over the meat. Repeat the layering to make 3 layers of filling topped with pasta sheets. Press down to compress the layers slightly. Pour the remaining 1 cup (250 ml) of sauce over the pasta and sprinkle with the remaining 1 cup (100 g) of Parmesan.

9. Bake, uncovered, for about 1 hour, until the top is golden brown and the sides are bubbling. Let stand 10 to 15 minutes before serving.

SERVES 6 TO 8

Note: The sausage, meatballs, cheese mixture, and sauce can be prepared and refrigerated, covered, up to 2 days in advance.

Fresco's Vegetable Lasagne

BÉCHAMEL SAUCE
2½ cups (630 ml) milk
1 shallot, coarsely chopped
⅛ teaspoon freshly grated nutmeg
3 tablespoons (45 g) unsalted butter
3 tablespoons unbleached all-purpose (plain) flour
Salt to taste

LASAGNE
6 tablespoons (90 g) unsalted butter
8 cups (900 g) julienned onions (about 2 pounds)
Salt to taste
3 tablespoons (45 ml) olive oil
1½ pounds (675 g) fresh spinach, trimmed, washed, and dried, with
    some moisture left clinging to the leaves
2 cups (280 g) diced fresh whole-milk mozzarella cheese
1 cup (230 g) fresh ricotta cheese
3 cups (300 g) freshly grated Parmesan cheese (about 11 ounces)
2 large eggs
¼ cup (10 g) chopped fresh flat-leaf parsley
Freshly ground black pepper to taste
1 pound (450 g) fresh pasta sheets or 8 ounces (230 g) dried lasagne sheets
2½ cups (565 g) canned crushed tomatoes
2 cups julienned Roasted Red Peppers (page 168)
1⅓ cups (340 g) drained and chopped olive-oil-marinated artichoke
    hearts (12 ounces)

1. To make the béchamel sauce, combine 2 cups (500 ml) of the milk, the shallot, and nutmeg in a small saucepan and bring to a boil over medium heat. Reduce the heat and simmer, uncovered, for about 5 minutes. Cover and set aside to keep hot.

2. In another saucepan, melt the butter over medium-low heat. Add the flour and, using a wooden spoon, stir until the flour absorbs the butter and

This vegetable lasagne is one of our favorites, and while it's terrific in the wintertime, it's also good in the summer or early fall when there are lots of vegetables you can use in place of the spinach. Try an equal amount of kale, Swiss chard, sliced zucchini or summer squash (vegetable marrow), or chopped broccoli and sauté them until al dente.

Most of our lasagnes include béchamel sauce, which we like because of the richness it adds, but you can leave it out. Both fresh and dried pasta sheets work well in this recipe. In fact, if you assemble the lasagne the day before cooking it, you are probably better off using dried sheets, which don't get as sticky as the fresh do when allowed to sit overnight in the refrigerator.

(continued on page 139)

forms a roux. Continue stirring for 2 to 3 minutes longer while the mixture bubbles and thickens.

3. Slowly pour the hot milk into the flour, whisking continuously to prevent lumps. Bring the sauce to a boil over medium heat. Reduce the heat and simmer for 2 to 3 minutes, until smooth and thickened. Season to taste with salt.

4. Strain through a fine sieve into a bowl or glass measuring cup. Add as much of the remaining ½ cup (120 ml) milk as necessary to make 2 cups (500 ml), whisking well to incorporate. Set aside, covered, until ready to use (see Note).

5. To prepare the lasagne, melt the butter in a large skillet over medium heat. Add the onions and cook, stirring often, for about 45 minutes, until softened and beginning to caramelize. Season to taste with salt and set aside until ready to use.

6. In a large sauté pan or deep skillet, heat the olive oil over medium heat. Add the spinach, stir, cover, and cook for 3 to 4 minutes, until well wilted. Season to taste with salt. Drain in a colander and then squeeze to remove excess moisture. Spread out on paper towels (kitchen paper) to cool. When cool, chop coarsely.

7. In a bowl, combine the mozzarella, ricotta, 2 cups (200 g) of the Parmesan, the eggs, and parsley. Stir well and season to taste with salt and pepper.

8. If using dried lasagne, bring a large pot of lightly salted water to a boil and cook the pasta for 8 to 10 minutes, until barely al dente. Drain and separate the sheets to cool. If using fresh pasta, do not cook it before assembling the lasagne.

9. Preheat the oven to 375°F (190°C).

10. In an 8 × 12-inch (20 × 30.5-cm) baking pan that is at least 2 inches (5 cm) deep, spread 1 cup (230 g) of the tomatoes. Lay a third of the pasta sheets over the tomatoes, overlapping slightly and trimming if necessary to fit.

11. Spread half the cheese mixture over the pasta. Top with half of the onions, half of the spinach, half of the peppers, and end with half of the artichokes. Drizzle ½ cup (120 ml) of the béchamel sauce over the vegetables and then spoon ½ cup (115 g) of the tomatoes over the sauce. Top with a third of the lasagne sheets. Repeat layering with the cheese, vegetables, sauce, and tomatoes, ending with the pasta.

(continued on page 140)

12. Spread the remaining béchamel sauce and tomatoes over the pasta and sprinkle with the remaining 1 cup (100 g) of Parmesan.

13. Bake, uncovered, for 35 to 40 minutes, until the top is golden brown. Let the lasagne stand for 10 to 15 minutes before serving.

SERVES 6 TO 8

Note: The béchamel sauce, onions, and spinach can be cooked, cooled, covered, and refrigerated up to 2 days in advance. Before using the chilled béchamel, thin it slightly by whisking in 3 to 4 tablespoons (50 to 60 ml) of milk if necessary.

You can substitute one 10-ounce (280-g) package of frozen spinach for the fresh. Let it thaw and then squeeze out all the moisture before sautéing it.

Chicken and Spinach Lasagne

This is a white lasagne, made without tomato sauce. It is sure to please those who like a little meat but don't want heavy red meat in their lasagne. We use a whole roasted chicken to get the white and dark meat, but if you prefer to use only chicken cutlets; they work well and reduce the fat a little.

BÉCHAMEL SAUCE
3 cups (750 ml) milk
1 shallot, coarsely chopped
¼ teaspoon freshly grated nutmeg
4½ tablespoons (70 g) unsalted butter
4½ tablespoons (40 g) unbleached all-purpose (plain) flour
Salt to taste

LASAGNE
5 tablespoons (75 g) unsalted butter
8 cups julienned (900 g) onions (about 2 pounds)
3 tablespoons (45 ml) olive oil
*1½ pounds (675 g) fresh spinach, trimmed, washed, and dried with some
    moisture left clinging to the leaves (see Note)*
2 cups (280 g) diced fresh mozzarella cheese
1 cup (230 g) fresh ricotta cheese
3 cups (300 g) freshly grated Parmesan cheese (about 11 ounces)
3 large eggs
¼ cup (10 g) chopped fresh flat-leaf parsley
Kosher salt and freshly ground black pepper to taste
1 pound (450 g) fresh pasta sheets or 8 ounces (230 g) dried lasagne sheets

½ cup (120 ml) heavy (double) cream
4 cups (675 g) roasted, boned, and shredded chicken

1. To make the béchamel sauce, combine 2½ cups (630 ml) of the milk, the shallot, and nutmeg in a small saucepan and bring to a boil over medium heat. Reduce the heat and simmer, uncovered, for about 5 minutes. Cover and set aside to keep hot.

2. In another saucepan, melt the butter over medium-low heat. Add the flour and, using a wooden spoon, stir until the flour absorbs the butter and forms a roux. Continue stirring for 2 to 3 minutes longer while the mixture bubbles and thickens.

3. Slowly pour the hot milk into the flour, whisking continuously to prevent lumps. Bring the sauce to a boil over medium heat. Reduce the heat and simmer for 2 to 3 minutes, until smooth and thickened. Season to taste with salt.

4. Strain through a fine sieve into a bowl or glass measuring cup. Add as much of the remaining ½ cup milk (120 ml) as necessary to make 2½ cups (630 ml), whisking well to incorporate. Set aside, covered, until ready to use (see Note).

5. To prepare the lasagne, heat the butter in a large skillet over medium heat until melted. Add the onions and cook, stirring often, for 25 to 30 minutes, until softened and beginning to caramelize. Season to taste with salt and set aside until ready to use.

6. In a large sauté pan or deep skillet, heat the olive oil over medium heat. Add the spinach, stir, cover, and cook for 3 to 4 minutes, until wilted. Season to taste with salt. Drain in a colander and then squeeze to remove excess moisture. Spread out on paper towels (kitchen paper) to cool. When cool, chop coarsely.

7. In a small bowl, combine the mozzarella, ricotta, 2 cups (200 g) of the Parmesan, the eggs, and parsley. Stir well and season to taste with salt and pepper.

8. If using dried lasagne, bring a large pot of lightly salted water to a boil and cook the pasta for 8 to 10 minutes, until barely al dente. Drain and separate the sheets to cool. If using fresh pasta, do not cook it before assembling the lasagne.

9. Preheat the oven to 350°F (175°C).

(continued on page 142)

Chicken and Spinach Lasagne
(*continued from page 141*)

10. In a 9 × 13-inch (23 × 33-cm) baking pan that is at least 2 inches (5 cm) deep, spread the cream over the bottom, tilting the pan if necessary to spread evenly. Lay a quarter of the pasta sheets over the cream, overlapping slightly and trimming if necessary to fit.

11. Spread a third of the cheese mixture evenly over the pasta. Top with a third of the onions, a third of the spinach, and a third of the chicken. Drizzle ¾ cup (180 ml) of the béchamel sauce over the chicken. Spread a third of the cheese mixture evenly over the pasta. Top with a third of the onions, a third of the spinach, and a third of the chicken. Drizzle ¾ cup (180 ml) of the béchamel sauce over the chicken. Repeat the process, ending with the pasta sheets. Press down to compress the layers slightly. Pour the remaining béchamel evenly over the pasta and sprinkle with the remaining 1 cup (100 g) of Parmesan.

12. Bake, uncovered, for 1 hour, until the top is golden brown and the sides are bubbling. Let stand 10 to 15 minutes before serving.

SERVES 6 TO 8

Note: The béchamel sauce, cheese mixture, onions, spinach, and chicken can be prepared and refrigerated, covered, up to 2 days in advance. Before using the chilled béchamel, thin it slightly by whisking in 3 to 4 tablespoons (50 to 60 ml) of milk if necessary.

Use leftover roasted chicken or roast two 1-pound (450-g) breasts with the bone in. The breasts will yield about 1 pound of meat when pulled off the bone. You can substitute one 10-ounce (280-g) package of frozen spinach for the fresh. Let it thaw and then squeeze out all the moisture before sautéing it.

Fennel-Crusted Pork Tenderloin with Roasted-Garlic Mashed Potatoes and Fresh Applesauce

SPICE CRUST
3 tablespoons fennel seeds
1 teaspoon salt
1 tablespoon black peppercorns

(*continued on page 144*)

(continued from page 142)

Pork tenderloin has very little fat, so we use a crust of spices to help retain its moisture, as well as add great flavor as it cooks. The spice mixture can be made well ahead of time and stored in an airtight container. We've used it on chicken, pork chops, and a crown roast. The pork roast is served with applesauce, which might be a cliché, but there's a reason for it: the two are really delicious together.

PORK

Three 1-pound (450-g) pork tenderloins, trimmed if necessary
1 tablespoon olive oil
3 tablespoons (45 g) unsalted butter, softened

Applesauce (recipe follows)
Roasted-Garlic Mashed Potatoes (recipe follows)

1. To make the spice crust, combine the fennel seeds, salt, and peppercorns in a blender. Process until ground, making sure no fennel seeds are left whole. Transfer to a large plate or work surface.

2. Preheat the oven to 500°F (260°C).

3. To prepare the pork, roll the tenderloins in the spice mixture, coating evenly on all sides.

4. In a large sauté pan, heat the olive oil over medium-high heat until very hot. Add the tenderloins and brown for 2 to 3 minutes, turning, until lightly browned on all sides.

5. Transfer to a roasting pan and roast for 10 to 12 minutes, until the internal temperature reaches 160°F (72°C) for medium. Remove from the oven and set aside to rest for 3 to 4 minutes. Lift the pork from the pan, carve into ½-inch-thick (1.3-cm) slices, and arrange on a serving platter.

6. Add the butter to the roasting pan and swirl to melt and mix with the pan drippings. Spoon over the pork. Serve the pork with applesauce and mashed potatoes.

SERVES 6

Note: The spice mixture for the crust can be stored in an airtight container in a cool, dark place for up to 3 months.

Applesauce

3 pounds (1.4 kg) firm, tart apples, quartered and cored
  (8 to 9 medium apples)
½ cup (100 g) sugar
Two 3-inch (7.5-cm) cinnamon sticks

1. In a large, nonreactive saucepan, combine the apples, sugar, cinnamon sticks, and 1 cup (250 ml) water. Bring to a simmer over medium heat. Reduce the heat to medium-low and simmer gently, uncovered, for about 1½ hours, stirring occasionally, until the sauce is thickened. Remove and discard the cinnamon sticks.

2. Push the sauce through a fine sieve or food mill. Transfer to a ceramic or glass container, cover, and refrigerate for at least 2 hours, until chilled, or for up to 1 week.

MAKES ABOUT 3 CUPS

Roasted-Garlic Mashed Potatoes

2 pounds (900 g) small red potatoes, cut into 1-inch (2.5-cm) chunks but
  not peeled
1 cup (250 ml) heavy (double) cream
6 tablespoons (90 g) unsalted butter
½ cup (230 g) Roasted Garlic puree (page 168)
Kosher salt to taste

1. Put the potatoes in a saucepan and add enough cold water to cover them by 3 inches (7.5 cm). Bring to a boil over high heat and cook, uncovered, for 15 to 20 minutes, until fork-tender. Drain the potatoes and set aside.

2. In a saucepan, combine the cream and butter and heat over medium heat to melt the butter. Raise the heat and bring the cream to a boil. Add the potatoes, mashing them with a fork as they are mixed with the cream. Do not mash them too much; they should be a little lumpy. Stir in the garlic, season to taste with salt, and serve hot.

SERVES 6

We serve these potatoes with everything—veal chops, grilled vegetables, fish—but we especially like them with Fennel-Crusted Pork Tenderloin (page 142). Roasted garlic has a milder flavor than other garlic and so does not overpower the potatoes but instead enhances them. If you prefer, you can leave out the garlic and rely on the butter and cream to give these potatoes their superb flavor and texture.

There's a very strong, very robust beef flavor to this dish, making it warming, hearty fare for the winter. In Italy a similar dish is called risotto de secolle. Secolle *is the meat from between the rib bones of the steer, which is not available in the United States. To replicate the flavor, we braise a brisket of beef. Be sure to read the text beside the recipe for* Risotto with Garlic Sausage, Tomatoes, and Arugula *on page 99 to learn the best way to make risotto.*

Risotto with Braised Beef

BEEF

One 10-ounce (280-g) beef brisket
Kosher salt and freshly ground black pepper to taste
1 tablespoon olive oil
1 medium onion, julienned
1 large clove garlic, chopped
1 cup (250 ml) dry white wine
2 cups (500 ml) Beef Stock (page 171)

RISOTTO

3½ cups (870 ml) Beef Stock (page 171)
1½ cups (375 ml) braising liquid from beef
6 tablespoons (90 ml) olive oil
½ cup (55 g) finely grated carrots (see Note)
½ cup (55 g) finely grated onions (see Note)
2 tablespoons chopped garlic
½ teaspoon crushed red pepper flakes
2 cups (340 g) arborio or carnaroli rice
⅓ cup (80 ml) dry white wine
½ cup (55 g) freshly grated Parmesan cheese
Kosher salt and freshly ground black pepper to taste
1 tablespoon brandy
2 tablespoons chopped fresh flat-leaf parsley
3 tablespoons (45 ml) extra-virgin olive oil

1. To braise the beef, preheat the oven to 400°F (200°C).

2. Season the beef with salt and pepper. In a Dutch oven or ovenproof stockpot, heat the oil over medium-high heat and then sear the beef for 5 to 6 minutes on each side, until browned.

3. Pour any excess oil from the pot and add the onions, garlic, wine, and stock. Roast, covered, for about 2 hours, or until the meat is fork-tender and almost falling apart. Transfer the beef to a platter, cover, and refrigerate for several hours, until cool. Pour the braising liquid into a container, cover, and refrigerate until ready to make the risotto.

4. Using a knife, shred the beef and set aside.

5. To make the risotto, in a large saucepan, combine the stock and reserved braising liquid and bring to a simmer over medium-high heat. Reduce the heat to medium or medium-low to keep the liquid barely simmering.

6. In a large, heavy stockpot, heat the olive oil over medium heat. Add the carrots, onions, garlic, and red pepper flakes and cook, covered, for 10 to 12 minutes, until the vegetables are softened but not brown.

7. Raise the heat to medium-high, add the rice, and stir for about 15 seconds, or until the grains are well coated with oil.

8. Add the wine and stir constantly, being careful to scrape the sides and bottom of the pan gently so that the rice does not stick. When the wine is almost gone, add ½ cup (120 ml) of the simmering stock and stir until the stock is nearly absorbed by the rice. Repeat, adding ½ cup (120 ml) of the stock after each preceding amount has been almost absorbed, until all the stock is used. The entire process will take 17 or 18 minutes. It is very important to stir the rice constantly for even cooking and a creamy texture, although it will remain al dente.

9. When all the broth has been used, add the reserved beef and the Parmesan, stirring gently to mix. Cook for about 3 minutes, or until the flavors blend. Season with salt and pepper to taste.

10. Remove from the heat and add the brandy. Stir vigorously for 30 seconds to incorporate the brandy. Divide the risotto among 6 plates and garnish each one with chopped parsley and a drizzle of extra-virgin olive oil.

SERVES 6

Note: Use a food processor to grate the carrots and onions, grating one vegetable at a time. The shredded beef and the braising liquid can be refrigerated in separate containers for 2 to 3 days or frozen for up to 2 months in tightly sealed containers.

Most likely, there are as
many versions of osso buco
as there are cooks in Italy.
Every restaurant serves it,
and each one is slightly
different. At our restaurant
we experimented with a few
variations before deciding on
this one. It requires some
advance preparation, but
once the meat is in the oven,
your job is complete. When
it's cooked, the meat is very
tender and goes well with
orzo, roasted potatoes,
Roasted-Garlic Mashed
Potatoes (page 145), or
Creamy Polenta (page 108).

Osso Buco

½ ounce (15 g) dried porcini mushrooms
½ pound (230 g) pancetta, coarsely chopped
6 tablespoons (90 ml) olive oil
1 large onion, finely grated (see Note)
½ pound (230 g) carrots, finely grated
1 small bulb fennel, trimmed and finely grated
3 tablespoons minced garlic
6 veal shanks, each about 2 inches (5 cm) thick, halved
Salt and freshly ground black pepper to taste
2 cups (500 ml) Veal Stock (page 171) or Chicken Stock (page 171)
1 cup (250 ml) dry red wine
1 cup (230 g) canned crushed tomatoes
1 tablespoon unsalted butter
½ pound (230 g) fresh wild mushrooms, such as shiitakes or chanterelles,
    stemmed and sliced (about 3 cups)

1. In a small bowl, cover the dried mushrooms with ½ cup (120 ml) warm water and set aside for about 30 minutes to plump. Strain any remaining soaking water and set aside.

2. Preheat the oven to 350°F (175°C).

3. In a nonstick skillet, cook the pancetta over medium heat just until the fat is rendered. Discard the fat and set the pancetta aside.

4. In a large skillet, heat 3 tablespoons of the olive oil over low heat. Add the onion, carrots, fennel, and garlic and cook very slowly for about 20 minutes, stirring often, until very soft. Transfer the vegetables to a roasting pan large enough to hold the veal shanks in a single layer.

5. Season the shanks generously with salt and pepper. In the same large skillet, heat the remaining 3 tablespoons of oil over medium-high heat until very hot. Sear the shanks for 3 to 5 minutes on each side, until browned. You may have to do this in batches. As they brown, transfer the shanks to the roasting pan, placing them on top of the vegetables.

6. Add the plumped porcini mushrooms, strained soaking water, and pancetta

to the roasting pan. In a small bowl, combine the stock, wine, and crushed tomatoes and stir to mix. Pour over the shanks to cover evenly. Cover the pan with foil and roast for 1½ hours. Remove the foil and continue roasting for about 1 hour longer, until the meat is tender. If necessary, cook the shanks longer, checking for doneness every 15 minutes.

7. Meanwhile, in a nonstick skillet, heat the butter over medium-low heat until melted. Add the fresh mushrooms and cook for 10 to 15 minutes, until tender. Set aside.

9. Using a spatula, transfer the shanks to a plate. Take care that they do not fall apart. Transfer the vegetables and cooking liquid to a saucepan. Skim the fat from the surface and cook over medium-high heat until reduced to 3 cups. Add the sautéed mushrooms and stir until heated through. Serve the sauce with the veal shanks.

SERVES 6

Note: *Use a food processor to grate the onion, carrots, and fennel, grating one vegetable at a time.*

Milanese Veal

2 cups (280 g) all-purpose (plain) flour
6 large eggs
¾ cup (85 g) freshly grated Parmesan cheese
3 cups (170 g) unseasoned toasted bread crumbs
1 teaspoon kosher salt
1 teaspoon garlic powder
¼ cup (10 g) chopped fresh flat-leaf parsley
Twelve 3-ounce (85-g) veal cutlets, pounded thin
2 to 3 cups (500 to 750 ml) olive oil or other vegetable oil

1. Put the flour in a shallow bowl. In another shallow bowl, combine the eggs, ¼ cup (30 g) of the cheese, and 3 tablespoons of water and beat with a fork until blended. In a third shallow bowl, mix together the bread crumbs, salt, remaining ½ cup (55 g) cheese, garlic powder, and parsley. Arrange the bowls on a work surface so that they are lined up next to each other.

In many respects, this is the perfect entree, which explains why it is such a common preparation in Italy. Usually it's made with veal, but thin-pounded chicken or lamb works well too. The breading mixture always includes bread crumbs, Parmesan, and parsley, and the cutlets are breaded and pan-fried in oil. While this is the first step to making veal or chicken parmigiana (blanketed with tomato sauce and grated cheese), we like it just like this, served with a simple salad.

(continued on page 150)

2. Carefully dip a cutlet into the flour and turn to coat both sides. Tap off the excess flour and then dip the cutlet into the egg mixture, turning to coat it well. Finally, dip it into the bread crumb mixture and coat both sides well, gently tapping off any excess. Transfer to a plate and set aside while repeating with the remaining cutlets.

3. Line another plate with a double thickness of paper towels (kitchen paper).

4. In a large, heavy skillet, heat 2 cups (500 ml) of the oil over medium-high heat until hot; a few bread crumbs sprinkled into the oil should sizzle immediately. Put 2 to 3 cutlets into the pan in a single layer and cook for 2 to 3 minutes on each side, until golden brown. Transfer to the towel-lined plate. Repeat with the remaining cutlets. If necessary, add more oil, taking care that it reaches a high temperature before adding the cutlets. Do not cook the cutlets over high heat or they might burn. Serve immediately or let the cutlets cool to room temperature before serving.

SERVES 6

Note: If you prefer to serve the cutlets at room temperature, serve them as soon as they reach that temperature. They should not be refrigerated or they will lose their crispness. You can substitute chicken or lamb for veal in the recipe.

Venetian Calves' Liver

5 to 6 tablespoons (75 to 90 ml) olive oil
2 pounds (900 g) onions, julienned (about 6 cups)
½ pound (230 g) pancetta, cut into ¼-inch (6-mm) slices
¼ cup (35 g) all-purpose (plain) flour
2½ to 3 pounds (1.1 to 1.4 kg) calves' liver, sliced into 12 thin pieces
(each about ⅛ inch/3 mm thick)
Kosher salt and freshly ground black pepper to taste
¼ cup (60 ml) brandy
1 cup (250 ml) Veal Stock (page 171) or Chicken Stock (page 171)
2 teaspoons finely chopped fresh rosemary
1 tablespoon chopped fresh flat-leaf parsley
2 tablespoons (30 g) unsalted butter

1. In a large sauté pan, heat 2 tablespoons of the oil over medium-low heat. Add the onions and cook for 20 to 25 minutes, stirring frequently, until soft and caramelized.

2. Meanwhile, in another large sauté pan, cook the pancetta over medium heat for about 20 minutes, or until most of the fat is rendered and the pancetta is crispy. Remove with a slotted spoon, drain on paper towels (kitchen paper), and set aside.

3. Spread the flour on a flat plate or work surface. Season the liver with salt and pepper and then dredge lightly in the flour, coating both sides.

4. In a clean large sauté pan, heat 2 more tablespoons of the oil over medium-high heat until it begins to smoke. Cook the liver, a few slices at a time, for 1 to 1½ minutes on each side, turning with tongs, until browned around the edges. Take care that the oil does not spatter. Reduce the heat to medium if necessary to prevent burning. Remove the liver from the pan and set it aside while continuing to cook all the liver, adding more oil as necessary. Remove the last batch of liver from the pan and set aside.

5. Put the cooked onions and pancetta in the pan used to cook the liver and cook over medium-high heat for about 1 minute, until heated through.

6. Remove the pan from the heat and pour in the brandy. Return the pan to the heat and simmer for 1 to 2 minutes, until the alcohol cooks off. (If you are using a gas stove, the brandy may flame briefly.)

7. Add the stock, rosemary, and parsley, stir well, and cook for 8 to 10 minutes, until the liquid is reduced by half. Add the butter and stir gently until it is incorporated. Return the liver to the pan, season with salt and pepper if necessary, and serve.

SERVES 6

Note: *For best results, partially freeze the liver before slicing it. The onions and pancetta can be prepared in advance. Depending on their temperature, it may take more than a minute to heat them through, as described in step 5.*

At the restaurant we use an electric slicer to cut the liver into thin pieces. In Italy chefs and home cooks slice it by hand, and it's amazing how thin they get it. That's the secret to this recipe: very thin slices of liver. Do it yourself or ask the butcher to slice it for you. Although we added pancetta, we otherwise left this recipe just as it's prepared in Italy, where it tends to be a family meal rather than a restaurant dish.

Bollito Misto

1 large tomato, cut into wedges
1 large onion
1 large carrot
1 large rib celery
3 bay leaves
2 tablespoons chopped fresh flat-leaf parsley
2 pounds (900 g) beef brisket
1 tablespoon kosher salt, plus more to taste
1 teaspoon whole black peppercorns
1 pound (450 g) cotechino (garlic) sausage
One 2½-pound (1.13-kg) whole chicken
1 pound (450 g) baking potatoes, peeled and cut into large pieces
1 pound (450 g) carrots, peeled and cut into 2-inch pieces
Freshly ground black pepper to taste
Extra-virgin olive oil
Green Sauce (recipe follows)
Mustard Fruits (recipe follows)

1. In a Dutch oven or other large pot, combine the tomato, onion, carrot, celery, bay leaves, and 1 tablespoon of the parsley and add enough water to cover by 3 to 4 inches. You may need as much as a gallon (4 l). Bring to a boil over high heat and add the brisket, 1 tablespoon of salt, and the peppercorns. Reduce the heat and simmer for about 1½ hours, skimming off the foam that rises to the surface several times.

2. Meanwhile, in a large saucepan or small stockpot, combine the sausage and 2 quarts (2 l) water and bring to a boil over high heat. Reduce the heat and simmer, partially covered, for about 1 hour, until tender. Lift the sausage from the pot and set aside to cool. When cool enough to handle, remove the casings and slice the sausage.

3. Remove the giblets from the chicken and discard or reserve for another use. Cut the chicken into quarters and, when the brisket has cooked for 1½ hours, add the chicken to the pot with the brisket, making sure it is fully submerged.

Clockwise from bottom: Bollito Misto; Mustard Fruits
(recipe on page 155); Green Sauce (recipe on page 154)

(continued on page 154)

This is a very traditional Italian dish that nearly always becomes a two- or three-day meal. After the first day the meat is cut from the bones and used as a filling for tortellini or as the base for pasta sauce. On the third day the broth is used to make soup. In some ways bollito misto *is similar to New England boiled dinner: large pieces of meat and vegetables are cooked simply in a big pot. In Italy it may include tongue and pig or cow knuckle, but for the home cook we suggest chicken, garlic sausage, and brisket. You can substitute another Italian sausage for the cotechino, figuring on about half a sausage link for each serving.*

Add more water if necessary to cover. Bring to a simmer over medium-high heat and cook, partially covered, for about 1 hour longer, until the brisket is tender and the chicken is cooked through. Lift the brisket and the chicken from the pot and set aside. Reserve 2 cups (500 ml) of the broth. Reserve the remaining broth for other uses (see Note).

4. In a large saucepan, combine the potatoes, carrots, and reserved brisket cooking broth. The broth should cover the vegetables; if not, add more water or broth. Bring to a boil over high heat and cook for 15 to 18 minutes, until the vegetables are tender. Drain and transfer the vegetables to a serving bowl. Season with salt and pepper, sprinkle with the remaining 1 tablespoon parsley, and drizzle with olive oil.

5. Serve the vegetables with the brisket, chicken, and sausage and the Green Sauce and Mustard Fruits on the side.

SERVES 6

Note: The leftover broth makes delicious soup. Freeze it for a later use, or use it with any leftover meat from this recipe to make soup.

Green Sauce

The condiments served with Bollito Misto are traditional as well. The Green Sauce includes anchovies, which can be omitted if you prefer.

(photograph on page 152)

½ cup fresh bread cubes, crust removed (about 1 slice bread)
1½ cups (60 g) roughly chopped fresh flat-leaf parsley leaves
1 tablespoon drained capers
4 oil-cured anchovy fillets, patted dry
2 hard-cooked egg yolks
¼ cup (60 ml) red wine vinegar
¾ cup (180 ml) extra-virgin olive oil
Kosher salt to taste

1. Place the bread in a bowl and pour 3 tablespoons (45 ml) boiling water over it. Let stand for 10 minutes and then squeeze out any excess moisture.

2. Transfer to the bowl of a food processor. Add the parsley, capers, anchovies, egg yolks, vinegar, oil, and salt to taste and process until smooth. Taste and add more salt if necessary. Serve with Bollito Misto.

MAKES ABOUT 1½ CUPS (375 ML)

Note: This sauce can be refrigerated for up to 3 days. Cover the container with plastic wrap resting directly on the surface of the sauce to prevent a film from forming.

Mustard Fruits

2 cups (500 ml) dry white wine
1 cup (200 g) sugar
2 tablespoons (30 ml) fresh lemon juice
1 Granny Smith (crisp, tart) apple, peeled, cored, and cut into wedges
1 Bartlett pear, peeled, cored, and cut into wedges
1 peach, peeled, pitted (stoned), and cut into wedges
3 plums, peeled, pitted (stoned), and cut into wedges
½ cup (70 g) dried apricots (about 2½ ounces)
1 tablespoon finely chopped lemon zest
2½ tablespoons hot mustard powder
1 large bay leaf

We simplified the Mustard Fruits recipe a little, calling for dried apricots because fresh apricots can be difficult to find.

(photograph on page 152)

1. In a large pot, combine the wine, 2 cups (500 ml) water, sugar, and lemon juice and bring to a boil over high heat. Add the apple wedges and cook for 2½ minutes, until somewhat transparent but still firm. Using a slotted spoon, remove the wedges from the liquid and set aside. Repeat the process with the pear, peach, plums, and apricots.

2. Add the lemon zest, mustard powder, and bay leaf to the cooking liquid. Reduce the heat and simmer, uncovered, for about 20 minutes, until it reduces to about 1½ (375 ml) cups.

3. Return the fruit to the pot and cook over high heat for about 6 minutes, until tender and the flavors blend. Remove from the heat and set aside to cool. Serve with Bollito Misto.

SERVES 6

Note: Once cooled, the fruits can be packed in lidded sterilized glass jars and refrigerated for up to 2 weeks.

Braised Short Ribs of Beef

¼ cup (60 ml) olive oil
6 pounds (2.7 kg) short ribs of beef, cut 2 inches (5 cm) wide
2 teaspoons salt, or to taste
Freshly ground black pepper to taste
6 ounces (170 g) pancetta, diced (about 1 cup)
1 cup (115 g) finely grated carrots (about 2 carrots) (see Note)
1 cup (115 g) finely grated onion (about 1 onion)
1 cup (115 g) finely grated fennel (1 trimmed bulb)
¼ cup chopped garlic (about 10 cloves)
1 tablespoon grated lemon zest
1 tablespoon grated orange zest
1½ cups (375 ml) tomato puree
1 cup (250 ml) red wine
1 cup (250 ml) Veal or Beef Stock (page 171)
1½ teaspoons crushed red pepper flakes

1. In a large, heavy skillet, heat the oil over medium-high heat. Season the short ribs with salt and pepper and put about a third of them into the skillet. Sear them for 2 to 3 minutes on each side, until browned, and transfer to a roasting pan. Sear the remaining ribs in batches, taking care not to crowd the pan with the ribs.

2. Reduce the heat to low, add the pancetta to the same skillet, and cook for 10 to 12 minutes, until the fat is rendered. Carefully pour off the fat and discard, keeping the pancetta in the skillet.

3. Add the carrots, onion, fennel, and garlic and cook, covered, for about 20 minutes, until the vegetables soften. Add the lemon and orange zest, tomato puree, wine, stock, and red pepper flakes. Season to taste with salt if necessary and continue to cook for about 5 minutes longer.

4. Preheat the oven to 375°F (190°C).

5. Pour the sauce over the ribs in the roasting pan, making sure they are nearly covered. If necessary, add more stock or water so that the liquid comes three-

Nothing could be simpler than this dish. This is one of our favorite braised entrees. It is similar to osso buco but tastes different because it is made with beef ribs rather than veal. You can buy the short ribs in any supermarket and, if it is easier, make the dish a day ahead of time. In fact, it tastes even better on the second day. And if you have leftover ribs, cut the meat off the bone and mix it into red sauce for a wonderful pasta sauce.

quarters of the way up the sides of the ribs. Cover tightly with aluminum foil and bake for 1½ hours. Remove the foil and bake for about 1 hour longer, until the ribs are very tender.

6. Transfer the ribs to a warm serving platter. Pour the sauce remaining in the pan into a saucepan, bring to a boil over medium-high heat, and cook until reduced to about 3 cups. Serve the ribs with the sauce.

SERVES 6

Note: Use a food processor to grate the carrots, onion, and fennel, grating one vegetable at a time.

Stewed Chicken and Sausage

One 3-pound (1.4-kg) chicken, cut into pieces and the breasts halved
Salt and freshly ground black pepper to taste
½ cup (120 ml) olive oil
6 hot or sweet Italian sausages (about 1 pound/450 g)
4 cups (450 g) julienned onions
2 cups (230 g) diced carrots
3 tablespoons chopped fresh garlic (about 8 cloves)
½ teaspoon crushed red pepper flakes, or to taste
2 cups (500 ml) Chicken Stock (page 171)
2 cups (500 ml) dry white wine
2 cups (500 ml) tomato puree
2 tablespoons minced fresh rosemary leaves
½ cup (85 g) golden raisins (sultanas)

1. Season the chicken pieces with salt and pepper. In a Dutch oven or large saucepan, heat the olive oil over medium-high heat. Add the chicken and sear for 3 to 4 minutes on each side, until golden brown. Remove the chicken from the pan and drain on a plate lined with paper towels (kitchen paper).

2. Add the sausage to the pan and cook for 3 to 4 minutes, turning, until browned. Remove the sausage and drain on a plate lined with paper towels.

This dish is typical of Italian home cooking. Nearly everyone who grew up in an Italian household, whether in Italy or elsewhere, remembers a chicken and sausage stewed dish. This one is a combination of Vincent's and Marion's versions. It's important to use really good Italian sausage, and if you prefer other vegetables, substitute those you like.

(continued on page 158)

Stewed Chicken and Sausage
(continued from page 157)

3. Reduce the heat to medium and add the onions, carrots, garlic, and red pepper flakes to the pan. Cook, stirring, for about 5 minutes, until the vegetables soften.

4. Add the stock, wine, tomato puree, rosemary, and raisins and stir to blend.

5. Return the chicken and sausage to the pot and stir to coat with the liquid. Bring the liquid to a boil over high heat. Reduce the heat and simmer, uncovered, for about 1½ hours, until the chicken is very tender and the sauce has thickened.

6. Season to taste with salt and pepper and serve.

SERVES 6

Cranberry Apple Tart with Hazelnut Crust

TART DOUGH
¾ pound (340 g) toasted hazelnuts (filberts), skins removed
3 cups (525 g) all-purpose (plain) flour, sifted
1½ cups (3 sticks/340 g) unsalted butter, at room temperature, cut into pieces
1½ cups (310 g) sugar
3 large egg yolks
Grated zest of 1 large orange (about 1½ tablespoons)
1½ tablespoons Grand Marnier liqueur
1 tablespoon ground cinnamon
¼ teaspoon ground nutmeg
¼ teaspoon salt

FILLING
3 pounds (1.4 kg) crisp, tart apples, such as Granny Smith, peeled, cored, and cut into thin wedges (about 3 cups)
1 cup (115 g) fresh cranberries, rinsed and dried
½ cup (100 g) sugar
1 teaspoon ground cinnamon

2 tablespoons unsalted butter, melted
2 tablespoons all-purpose flour
Unsweetened whipped cream, for garnish

1. To make the dough, place the nuts and ½ cup (70 g) of the flour in a food processor fitted with the metal blade and pulse 3 to 4 times, or until finely ground. Transfer to a large bowl.

2. Add the remaining 2½ cups flour and the butter, sugar, egg yolks, orange zest, Grand Marnier, cinnamon, nutmeg, and salt.

3. Using your fingertips, press the mixture together to form a cohesive dough and turn out onto a lightly floured surface. Roll into 2 equal-sized balls and flatten into discs. Wrap 1 disc in plastic wrap (cling film) and refrigerate for at least 1 hour. Wrap the other disc in plastic wrap and then aluminum foil and freeze for a later use.

4. To make the tart, preheat the oven to 350°F (175°C).

5. Using your fingertips, firmly press the dough into a 10-inch (25-cm) tart pan with a removable bottom, spreading it evenly over the bottom and up the sides of the pan so that it is about ¼ inch (6 mm) thick.

6. In a large bowl, combine the apples, cranberries, sugar, cinnamon, butter, and flour. Pour the filling into the unbaked tart shell, spreading it evenly to distribute the apples and cranberries to the edges of the tart shell.

7. Bake for about 1 hour, until the apples are golden, the fruit glistens, and the crust is golden brown. If the crust browns too much during baking, shield it with strips of foil. Cool on a wire rack. Serve with whipped cream.

SERVES 8 TO 12 AND MAKES ONE 10-INCH TART

Note: The dough for the crust can be made 1 day ahead and refrigerated. To use the extra dough, keep it frozen for up to 1 month and let it thaw completely in the refrigerator before using.

We love the combination of sweet apples and tart cranberries. Fruit tarts are common in Italy, but while the Italians never cook or bake with cranberries, they are so delicious here in the fall and winter, we have to include them on the menu. Hazelnuts are another ingredient commonly used in Italian cooking, and they add a wonderful dimension to the crust. The dough can be made a day ahead of time, or you can double or triple the recipe and keep it in the freezer to use later. We suggest serving this with unsweetened whipped cream, but for a richer topping, try the Mascarpone Whipped Cream on page 38. (photograph on page 126)

Panettone Bread Pudding

½ pound (230 g) panettone (see Note), cut into ½-inch (1.3-cm) cubes (about 4 cups)
2 cups (500 ml) heavy (double) cream
2 cups (500 ml) whole milk
6 large egg yolks
1 cup (200 g) plus 3 tablespoons sugar
2 tablespoons finely chopped orange zest
1 teaspoon pure vanilla extract
1 tablespoon unsalted butter
6 ounces (170 g) semisweet (dark) chocolate, coarsely chopped
Sweetened whipped cream, for garnish

1. Preheat the oven to 200°F (95°C).

2. Spread the panettone cubes in a single layer on a baking sheet or in a shallow baking dish and bake for 30 to 40 minutes, until dried out.

3. In a large bowl, combine the cream, milk, egg yolks, 1 cup of sugar, orange zest, and vanilla extract. Whisk gently until the sugar dissolves. Add the panettone to the bowl and set aside to soak for 30 minutes.

4. Increase the oven temperature to 350°F (175°C).

5. Rub the butter over the bottom and sides of a 2-quart (2-l) glass or ceramic baking dish about 8 × 12 inches (20 × 30.5 cm) and 2½ (4 cm) inches deep. Sprinkle the remaining 3 tablespoons of sugar over the butter.

6. Stir the chocolate into the panettone mixture and then pour the mixture into the baking dish. Set the dish in a larger pan and add enough hot water to come halfway up the sides of the dish. Bake for 45 to 50 minutes, until the surface is golden brown and firm and the custard is set. Remove from the water bath and set aside to cool for 20 minutes. Serve warm, garnished with whipped cream.

SERVES 6 TO 8

Note: Panettone is a traditional Italian fruit cake sold in Italian markets and specialty stores. One small commercially available cake is about 16 ounces.

Two-Layer Chocolate Cheesecake

½ pound (230 g) semisweet (dark) chocolate, coarsely chopped
½ cup (1 stick/115 g) unsalted butter
5 large eggs
1½ cups (310 g) sugar
1½ teaspoons pure vanilla extract
¼ teaspoon salt
1 cup (140 g) all-purpose (plain) flour
6 ounces (170 g) cream cheese, at room temperature
2 ounces (55 g) mascarpone cheese

Rich and seductively delicious, this dense chocolate cake topped with sweetened cheese is especially pretty served with fresh berries.

1. Preheat the oven to 325°F (165°C). Butter and flour a 10-inch (25-cm) springform pan, tapping out the excess flour.

2. In the top of a double boiler over barely simmering water, melt the chocolate and butter, stirring until smooth. Set aside to cool slightly.

3. In the bowl of an electric mixer set on medium-high speed, beat 4 of the eggs, 1 cup of the sugar, 1 teaspoon of the vanilla, and the salt for about 3 minutes, until the sugar dissolves and the batter is pale yellow. Turn the mixer to low and add the melted chocolate and butter. Beat for about 20 seconds, just until incorporated. Turn off the mixer and scrape down the sides of the bowl. Beat on low speed for 20 seconds longer. Using a spoon or rubber spatula, stir the flour into the batter until fully incorporated. Scrape the batter into the prepared springform pan.

4. In the bowl of an electric mixer set on medium-high speed, beat the cream cheese, mascarpone cheese, remaining 1 egg, remaining ½ teaspoon of vanilla, and remaining ½ cup of sugar until smooth.

5. Pour the cheese mixture in broad ribbons evenly over the cake batter. If necessary, use a rubber spatula to spread it very gently over the batter. Take care not to marbleize the two mixtures. Bake for 30 to 35 minutes, until the cake begins to set around the edges and a few bubbles appear on the surface of the cheese topping. (The cake will not look as though it is completely baked. Do not overbake.) Cool for 1 to 1½ hours on a wire rack. Run a knife around the edge of the cake and remove the sides of the pan. Serve immediately or refrigerate until ready to serve.

SERVES 6

grilled pizzas

We've been serving grilled pizzas at Fresco since we first opened. They cannot be baked in the oven like a more traditional pizza, so plan on firing up the grill. Vincent learned to make grilled pizzas while working at Al Forno Restaurant in Providence, Rhode Island, where owners George Germon and Johanne Killeen developed the technique. They taste quite different from other pizzas—the fire gives them a characteristic smokiness—and they are lighter too. The key to success is restraint with the toppings. There is no need to cover the crust entirely with tomato sauce, cheese, or anything else. Just dab on the toppings so that, with every bite, your mouth experiences a slightly new and exciting taste and texture. Too much topping can make the crust sodden, which would be a shame because a lot of the best flavor is in the grilled crust. We use the same dough for focaccia and for the bread salads.

Fresco Pizza Crust

1⅓ cups (330 ml) lukewarm water (105° to 110°F/40.5° to 43°C)
1 tablespoon molasses
1 teaspoon fresh yeast or 1 package (¼ ounce/7 g) active dry yeast
2½ tablespoons salt
2½ tablespoons olive oil, plus more for coating
2 cups (280 g) bread flour (see Note)
1½ cups (215 g) unbleached all-purpose (plain) flour
¼ cup (35 g) whole wheat (wholemeal) flour

1. In a large bowl, combine the water, molasses, and yeast and stir gently to mix. Set aside for about 5 minutes, until bubbling and foamy.

2. Add the salt and olive oil and stir to mix.

3. In another bowl, whisk together the flours. Add the flours to the yeast mixture and stir with a wooden spoon until a dough forms and pulls away from the sides of the bowl.

4. Form the dough into 2 or 6 balls and transfer to a lightly oiled bowl. Turn to coat with oil and then dab about 1 teaspoon of oil (¼ teaspoon for 6 balls) on top of each ball of dough. Cover the bowl with plastic wrap (cling film) and set aside at warm room temperature for about 20 minutes.

5. Prepare a charcoal or gas grill. Position the grilling rack 3 to 4 inches (7.5 to 10 cm) from the heat source. The coals should be very hot.

6. Oil a rimless baking sheet and flatten one ball of dough into a 10- to 12-inch (25- to 30-cm) or 5- to 6-inch (12.5- to 15-cm) round about ⅛ inch (3 mm) thick.

While a perfect circle is not important, it is important to maintain uniform thickness.

7. Using your fingertips, gently lift the dough and drape it onto the grill, guiding it carefully onto the rack. Within 1 minute it will puff slightly, the underside will stiffen, and grill marks will appear.

8. Using tongs, immediately flip the crust over onto the coolest part of the grill. Brush it with olive oil and proceed with one of the following recipes. Repeat the procedure with the other balls of dough.

MAKES TWO 10- TO 12-INCH OR SIX 5- TO 6-INCH PIZZAS; SERVES 6

Note: Bread flour is higher in gluten (protein) than all-purpose flour.

Pizza with Tomato-Mozzarella Salad

> 6 cups (1.4 kg) peeled, cored, and diced tomatoes
>   (about 6 large tomatoes)
> 2 cups (230 g) julienned red onions
> 1½ pounds (675 g) fresh mozzarella cheese,
>   cut into ¼-inch (6-mm) cubes
> ½ cup (20 g) chiffonade of fresh basil
> ½ cup (120 ml) extra-virgin olive oil
> ¼ cup (60 ml) balsamic vinegar
> Kosher salt and freshly ground black pepper
>   to taste
> 1 recipe Fresco Pizza Crust (page 162), divided
>   into 6 pieces

1. In a glass or ceramic bowl, combine the tomatoes, onions, mozzarella, and basil and toss gently. Add the oil and vinegar, season to taste with salt and pepper, and stir gently. If the ingredients are not at room temperature, set aside to bring to room temperature.

2. Complete grilling the pizza crusts by sliding them back to the edge of the hot section of the grill and rotating them for 2 to 3 minutes, until the bottoms are evenly golden brown.

3. Using a slotted spoon, spoon the tomato-mozzarella salad over the grilled pizza crust. Cut the pizzas and serve.

MAKES 6 ONE-SERVING PIZZAS

Grilled Pizza with Wild Mushrooms and Taleggio Cheese

(photograph on page 165)

> ¾ cup (180 ml) olive oil
> 1 tablespoon chopped garlic
> 3 pounds (1.4 kg) fresh wild mushrooms, such as
>   shiitakes, chanterelles, oysters, or cremini,
>   wiped clean and trimmed
> 2 tablespoons fresh thyme leaves
> Kosher salt to taste
> 1½ cups (160 g) grated romano cheese
> 1½ cups (180 g) grated fontina cheese
> 1¼ pounds (565 g) Taleggio cheese, rind removed
>   (see Note)
> 1 recipe Fresco Pizza Crust (page 162), divided
>   into 6 pieces

(continued on page 164)

Grilled Pizza with Wild Mushrooms and Taleggio Cheese

(continued from page 164)

1. Using 2 large sauté pans, heat 2 tablespoons of the oil in each pan over medium heat. Divide the garlic between the pans and cook until just browned. Divide the mushrooms and thyme between the pans and cook for 5 to 6 minutes, until the mushrooms release their moisture and cook down by about a third. Transfer to a colander to drain and cool. Season to taste with salt.

2. In a bowl, mix together the romano and fontina cheeses.

3. Spread about ½ cup (57 g) of the romano-fontina mixture over each pizza crust and then top each with about a cup of the mushrooms. Add a dollop of Taleggio cheese to each and then slide them back to the edge of the hot section of the grill. Rotate them for 3 to 4 minutes, until the bottoms are evenly golden brown. Cut the pizzas and serve.

MAKES 6 ONE-SERVING PIZZAS

Note: Taleggio is a soft, triple-cream cheese with a distinctive buttery flavor. Similar farmhouse cheeses are stracchino and crescenza. You can substitute Camembert or Brie, removing the rind and slicing the cheese very thin.

Grilled Pizza with Broccoli Rabe and Sausage

2 pounds (900 g) broccoli rabe
2 pounds (900 g) hot or mild Italian sausage
½ cup (120 ml) olive oil
2 tablespoons chopped garlic
½ teaspoon crushed red pepper flakes
Kosher salt to taste
2¼ cups (230 g) grated romano cheese
2¼ cups (280 g) grated fontina cheese
1 recipe Fresco Pizza Crust (page 162), divided into 6 pieces

1. In a large pot of boiling water, blanch the broccoli rabe over high heat for about 4 minutes. Using tongs or a slotted spoon, lift from the water and set aside to cool. When cool, chop coarsely.

2. Bring the water back to a boil over high heat and cook the sausage for about 15 minutes, until cooked through. Using tongs or a slotted spoon, remove the sausage from the water and immediately plunge in cold water to stop the cooking. When cool, remove the meat from the casings and crumble. (You will have about 6 cups of sausage.)

3. In a large sauté pan, heat the olive oil over medium-high heat and cook the garlic for about 30 seconds, until browned. Add the broccoli rabe and red pepper flakes to the pan and season to taste with salt. Cook for 6 to 7 minutes, until very tender.

4. In a bowl, mix together the romano and fontina cheeses.

Top to bottom: Grilled Pizza Margarita; Grilled Pizza with Wild Mushrooms and Taleggio Cheese (recipe on page 163)

5. Spread about ¾ cup (85 g) of the romano-fontina mixture over each pizza crust, top each with equal amounts of broccoli rabe and sausage, and then slide them back to the edge of the hot section of the grill. Rotate them for 3 to 4 minutes until the bottoms are evenly golden brown. Cut the pizzas and serve.

MAKES 6 ONE-SERVING PIZZAS

Grilled Pizza Margarita

3 cups (675 g) canned plum tomatoes in
   thick puree
¾ cup (30 g) chopped fresh basil
1 cup (250 ml) extra-virgin olive oil
2 tablespoons finely chopped garlic
2¼ cups (230 g) grated romano cheese
2¼ cups (280 g) grated fontina cheese
3 tablespoons chopped fresh flat-leaf parsley
1 recipe Fresco Pizza Crust (page 162), divided
   into 6 pieces

1. In a bowl, combine the tomatoes in puree, basil, ¼ cup of the olive oil (60 ml), and the garlic. Stir well and set aside at room temperature for up to 1 hour.

2. In a bowl, mix together the romano and fontina cheeses.

3. Spread about ¾ cup (85 g) of the romano-fontina mixture over each pizza crust and then dollop each with 8 to 10 tablespoons (120 to 150 ml) of the tomato sauce. Do not spread the sauce over the crust. Drizzle each pizza with about a tablespoon of the remaining olive oil and sprinkle each with parsley. Slide the crusts back to the edge of the hot section of the grill. Rotate them for 3 to 4 minutes, until the bottoms are evenly golden brown. Cut the pizzas and serve.

MAKES 6 ONE-SERVING PIZZAS

recipes for all seasons

We call these recipes for "all seasons" because they are the foundation on which we build so many of our dishes. On these pages you will find recipes for stocks, for pesto, for a basic tomato sauce, and for roasted garlic, among others. Because these recipes are so versatile, they are not ascribed to any one season.

We recommend that you utilize these home-made staples as often as you can. Make your own stock instead of relying on canned; oven-roast tomatoes to replace commercial sun-dried varieties; and take advantage of the garden's surplus crops of basil and peppers to make homemade pesto and roasted red peppers. Store stock and tomato sauce in pre-measured quantities in the freezer; keep roasted peppers, tomatoes, and garlic in the refrigerator. None of these preparations is difficult—only a little time-consuming—and the difference in quality is immediately apparent. Whenever you take the time to prepare these basics, you ensure that your cooking will be richer, more flavorful, and more expressive.

Potato and Zucchini Chips with Gorgonzola

(photograph on page 173)

When Marion visited her cousins in South Carolina, she tried potato chips with blue cheese at a local restaurant. When she returned to New York, she and Vincent devised their own version, making both potato and zucchini chips and serving them with creamy gorgonzola. It's become one of our most popular menu items—regardless of the season.

> *1 pound (450 g) large baking potatoes*
> *½ pound (230 g) large zucchini (courgettes)*
> *2 tablespoons all-purpose (plain) flour*
> *About 2 quarts (2 l) peanut oil, for frying*
> *   (see Note)*
> *4½ ounces (130 g) gorgonzola cheese, crumbled*
> *3 tablespoons (45 ml) heavy (double) cream*
> *Kosher salt to taste*

1. Peel the potatoes and, using a sharp knife, a food processor fitted with the metal blade, or a mandoline, cut them into thin slices. Immediately submerge them in a bowl filled with cold water to prevent discoloring.

2. Cut the zucchini into thin slices. (Do not put them in water.) Transfer the zucchini to a large bowl and toss with the flour.

3. In a large, deep, heavy sauté pan, pot, or deep-fat fryer, heat the oil to 325°F.

4. Lift about a third of the potatoes from the water and dry them well on paper towels (kitchen paper). Scatter them over the oil so that they do not clump and let them

fry for 1 minute. Gently stir the chips with a wooden spoon and continue to fry for about 2 minutes longer, until golden brown. Using a slotted spoon, lift the potatoes from the oil and drain on a double thickness of paper towels. Repeat with the remaining potatoes, frying them in 2 or 3 more batches and letting the oil regain the correct temperature between batches.

5. Let the oil regain the correct temperature, then fry the zucchini in 1 or 2 batches in the same way as the potatoes. Drain on paper towels.

6. In a small saucepan, combine the cheese and cream and heat over very low heat until the cheese melts. Stir until smooth.

7. Toss the potato and zucchini chips together in a large bowl or on a platter and salt lightly. (Keep in mind that the cheese provides saltiness.) Drizzle with the melted cheese and serve immediately.

SERVES 6

Note: Use a heavy pot when deep frying. You will need enough oil to fill the pan or pot to a depth of 2 to 3 inches (5 to 7.5 cm). Deep-fat fryers are equipped with a thermometer, which makes reading the temperature easy. If you don't have one, use a deep-fat frying thermometer. It's important that the oil be hot enough to fry the potatoes and zucchini; otherwise they will absorb oil during frying and be soggy.

Pesto

*½ cup (55 g) pine nuts (pine kernels)
   (about 2 ounces)
¾ cup (180 ml) plus 1 tablespoon extra-virgin
   olive oil
3 cloves garlic, coarsely chopped
4 cups (about 160 g) loosely packed fresh
   basil leaves
½ cup (55 g) freshly grated Parmesan cheese
Kosher salt to taste*

1. Preheat the oven to 350°F (175°C).

2. Spread the pine nuts in a single layer on a baking sheet and toast for 4 to 5 minutes, until fragrant and golden brown. Shake the pan once or twice during toasting and take care that the nuts do not burn. Transfer to a plate to cool.

3. In a blender or food processor fitted with the metal blade, combine ¾ cup of the olive oil, the garlic, 1 cup (40 g) of the basil, and the pine nuts. Process until nearly smooth. Add the remaining basil and process until nearly smooth. Add the cheese and pulse to combine. Season to taste with salt, pulsing 2 or 3 times just to mix. Use immediately or transfer to a glass or plastic container for storage. Top with the remaining 1 tablespoon olive oil, cover, and refrigerate.

MAKES ABOUT 1½ CUPS

Note: The pesto will keep for 2 to 3 days in the refrigerator and for up to 2 months in the freezer.

Rosemary Mayonnaise

2 large egg yolks
1 tablespoon Dijon mustard
2 teaspoons fresh lemon juice
3 dashes Tabasco or other hot pepper sauce
1 cup (250 ml) olive oil or corn oil
1½ tablespoons finely chopped fresh rosemary
Salt to taste

1. In a small bowl, combine the egg yolks, mustard, lemon juice, and Tabasco. Using a hand-held electric mixer or immersion blender set on medium speed, or using a wire whisk, add the oil by drops, whisking constantly, until the mixture begins to emulsify and nearly half the oil is incorporated. Do not add the oil too quickly.

2. Add the remaining oil in a steady stream, whisking constantly until all the oil is incorporated and the mayonnaise is thick. Stir in the rosemary and season to taste with salt. Cover and refrigerate for 2 to 3 hours.

MAKES ABOUT 1 CUP

Roasted Garlic

4 large, plump heads garlic, halved horizontally
  (on the equator)
4 teaspoons olive oil

1. Preheat the oven to 350°F (175°C).

2. To roast the garlic, lay the garlic halves on a sheet of aluminum foil and sprinkle with the olive oil. Wrap securely and bake for 45 to 50 minutes, until soft. Unwrap and cool slightly. Squeeze the garlic from the cloves and mash with a fork.

MAKES ABOUT 1 CUP

Note: You can make the puree ahead of time and store it in a jar with a tight-fitting lid. Pour a layer of olive oil over the garlic before securing the lid and refrigerating. If you prefer, you can halve, double, or triple the recipe and keep the extra on hand for other uses. The puree will keep for up to 1 week in the refrigerator and for up to a month in the freezer.

Roasted Red Peppers

12 red bell peppers (capsicums)
2 tablespoons extra-virgin olive oil

1. Preheat the oven to 500°F (260°C).

2. Rub the peppers with the oil and arrange them on a baking sheet. Roast for 10 to 15 minutes, until the skins turn dark and begin to blister. Transfer the peppers to a bowl and cover tightly with plastic wrap (cling film). Set aside for about 10 minutes to steam and cool.

3. When cool enough to handle, rub the skins from the peppers. Cut the peppers in half, scrape out the seeds, and prepare the peppers as required by a recipe.

MAKES ABOUT 3 CUPS CHOPPED PEPPERS

Note: Roasted peppers will keep in the refrigerator for up to a week if stored in a covered container.

Oven-Roasted Tomatoes

Use these wonderful tomatoes in place of commercial sun-dried tomatoes. They are more tender and still slightly juicy.

> 2 pints (675 g) cherry tomatoes, stemmed
> 2 tablespoons olive oil

1. Preheat the oven to 275°F (135°C).

2. In a large bowl, toss the tomatoes with the oil until completely coated. Spread the tomatoes in a single layer in a 9 × 13-inch (23 × 33-cm) baking pan and roast for 3½ hours. The tomatoes will shrivel and shrink to about half their original size.

3. Let the tomatoes cool in the pan. Use right away or cover and refrigerate for 4 to 5 days.

MAKES ABOUT 1 1/2 CUPS

Note: For longer storage, put the tomatoes in a glass jar with a tight-fitting lid. Cover them with olive oil and refrigerate for up to 2 weeks.

Basic Tomato Sauce

A good tomato sauce should have five ingredients: tomatoes, olive oil, garlic, basil, and salt. You can also add a few red pepper flakes. A simple sauce like this one lets you taste the tomatoes and can be used with pasta, in lasagne, on pizza, or in any number of dishes.

> 5 pounds (2.25 kg) plum tomatoes, cored
> ¾ cup (180 ml) olive oil
> 2 tablespoons chopped garlic
> 1½ teaspoons crushed red pepper flakes
> ½ cup (20 g) chopped fresh basil
> Salt to taste

1. Bring a large pot of water to a boil over high heat. Drop the tomatoes into the water and boil for 1 minute. Lift from the boiling water and immediately plunge into a bowl of cold water to stop the cooking. You will have to do this in several batches.

2. Slip the skins from the tomatoes, cut them in half, and gently squeeze out the seeds. Chop the tomatoes and set aside.

3. In a large, heavy saucepan, heat the oil over medium-low heat. Cook the garlic, stirring, for 3 to 5 minutes, until golden brown. Add the pepper flakes and cook 30 seconds longer.

4. Add the tomatoes and basil, raise the heat to medium, and simmer, uncovered, for about 1 hour, stirring often. Season to taste with salt and use immediately.

MAKES ABOUT 7 CUPS

Note: If you do not plan to use the sauce immediately, let it cool slightly and then cover and refrigerate for up to 3 days or freeze for up to 2 months.

Fresco Seasoning

We use this on Braised and Grilled Spareribs (page 72), but we also suggest using it on grilled vegetables, chicken, pork, and beef. While it overpowers most fish, a little sprinkled on shrimp or lobster, both of which are full flavored, is wonderful.

½ cup (55 g) plus 1 tablespoon dried oregano
5 tablespoons (70 g) kosher salt
4 tablespoons paprika
4 tablespoons ground fennel
3 tablespoons garlic powder
3 tablespoons onion powder
2 tablespoons cayenne pepper
4 teaspoons sugar

In a glass or plastic container with a tight-fitting lid, combine all the ingredients and shake or stir to mix. Store in a cool dark cupboard for up to 6 months.

MAKES ABOUT 2 CUPS

Fish Stock

½ cup (120 ml) olive oil
½ cup (55 g) sliced onion
½ cup (55 g) sliced celery
½ cup (55 g) sliced fennel
4 bay leaves
8 parsley stems
1 tablespoon black peppercorns
6 pounds (2.7 kg) lean fish bones, rinsed under cold water (see Note)
1 cup (250 ml) dry white wine
Kosher salt to taste

1. In a large stockpot, heat the oil over medium-high heat. Add the onion, celery, and fennel and cook, stirring, for 8 to 10 minutes, until the vegetables soften but do not caramelize. Add the bay leaves, parsley stems, peppercorns, and fish bones and cook, stirring, for 5 minutes.

2. Add the wine and cook for about 3 minutes, then add 3 quarts (3 l) water. Bring to a boil over high heat, reduce the heat to medium, and simmer for about 45 minutes, skimming any foam that rises to the surface.

3. Line a large colander with a double thickness of cheesecloth and strain the stock through the colander into a large bowl. Press on the solids to extract as much liquid as possible. Discard the solids and season the stock with salt. Use immediately or plunge the bowl into a larger bowl or sink full of ice and cold water to chill. Cover and refrigerate.

MAKES ABOUT 6 CUPS (1.5 L)

Note: Lean fish bones include bones from fish such as bass or pike. Ask the fishmonger for the bones and be sure to rinse them well. The stock keeps for up to 3 months in the freezer.

Beef or Veal Stock

10 pounds (4.5 kg) beef or veal bones
½ pound (230 g) celery, cut into large pieces
½ pound (230 g) carrots, cut into large pieces
½ pound (230 g) onions, cut into large pieces
6 ounces (170 g) fennel, cut into large pieces
3 tablespoons tomato paste
3 whole cloves garlic
10 black peppercorns
3 large bay leaves
4 sprigs fresh thyme
4 sprigs fresh flat-leaf parsley
Kosher salt to taste

1. Preheat the oven to 350°F (175°C).

2. Spread the bones in a large roasting pan so that they are in a single layer and roast for about 45 minutes, until the fat is rendered and the bones are lightly browned. Transfer the bones to a large stockpot. Pour or skim off fat from the roasting pan. Do not turn off the oven.

3. Put the celery, carrots, onions, fennel, and tomato paste in the same roasting pan and stir to mix. Roast for about 45 minutes, until the vegetables begin to brown. Transfer to the stockpot. Add the garlic, peppercorns, bay leaves, thyme, and parsley. Pour about 7 quarts (7 l) of water over the bones and vegetables.

4. Bring to a boil over high heat, reduce the heat to medium-low, and simmer gently for about 4 hours, skimming the foam that rises to the surface from time to time.

5. Line a large colander with a double thickness of cheesecloth and strain the stock through the colander into a large bowl. Press on the solids to extract as much liquid as possible, then discard the solids. Season with salt. Use immediately or plunge the bowl into a larger bowl or sink full of ice and cold water to chill. Cover and refrigerate.

MAKES ABOUT 2 QUARTS (2 L)

Note: You may have to order veal bones from the butcher. The stock keeps for up to 3 months in the freezer.

Chicken Stock

10 pounds (4.5 kg) chicken bones (including necks, backs, and wings), rinsed under cold water
½ pound (230 g) celery, cut into large pieces
½ pound (230 g) carrots, cut into large pieces
½ pound (230 g) onions, cut into large pieces
¼ pound (115 g) fennel, cut into large pieces
2 whole cloves garlic
10 black peppercorns
3 large bay leaves
1 sprig fresh thyme
1 sprig fresh flat-leaf parsley
Kosher salt to taste

1. In a large stockpot, combine the chicken bones with enough cold water to cover by 3 to 4 inches (7.5 to 10 cm). Bring to a boil over high heat. Drain the bones, discarding the water, and return them to the pot. Pour about 7 quarts (7 l) of cold water over the bones in the pot. Add the remaining ingredients except the salt.

2. Bring to a boil over high heat, reduce the heat to medium-low, and simmer gently for about 4 hours, skimming the foam that rises to the surface from time to time.

(continued on page 172)

3. Line a large colander with a double thickness of cheesecloth and strain the stock through the colander into a large bowl. Press on the solids to extract as much liquid as possible. Discard the solids and season the stock with salt. Use immediately or plunge the bowl into a larger bowl or sink full of ice and cold water to chill. Cover and refrigerate.

MAKES ABOUT 2 QUARTS (2 L)

Note: The stock keeps for up to 3 months in the freezer.

Duck Stock

10 pounds (4.5 kg) duck bones (including necks, backs, and wings), rinsed under cold water
½ pound (230 g) celery, cut into large pieces
½ pound (230 g) carrots, cut into large pieces
½ pound (230 g) onions, cut into large pieces
¼ pound (115 g) fennel, cut into large pieces
2 whole cloves garlic
10 black peppercorns
3 large bay leaves
1 sprig fresh thyme
1 sprig fresh flat-leaf parsley
Kosher salt to taste

1. Preheat the oven to 350°F (175°C).

2. Spread the bones in a large roasting pan so that they are in a single layer and roast for about 45 minutes, until the fat is rendered and the bones are lightly browned. Transfer the bones to a large stockpot.

3. Add enough cold water to the pot to cover the bones by 3 to 4 inches (7.5 to 10 cm). Bring to a boil over high heat. Drain the bones, discarding the water, and return them to the pot. Pour about 7 quarts (7 l) of cold water over the bones in the pot. Add the remaining ingredients except the salt.

4. Bring to a boil over high heat, reduce the heat to medium-low, and simmer gently for about 4 hours, skimming the foam that rises to the surface from time to time.

5. Line a large colander with a double thickness of cheesecloth and strain the stock through the colander into a large bowl. Press on the solids to extract as much liquid as possible. Discard the solids and season the stock with salt. Use immediately or plunge the bowl into a larger bowl or sink full of ice and cold water to chill. Cover and refrigerate.

MAKES ABOUT 2 QUARTS (2 L)

Note: The stock keeps for up to 3 months in the freezer.

Opposite: Potato and Zucchini Chips with Gorgonzola (recipe on page 166)

Tuscan Bread

2 tablespoons molasses
1¾ cups (430 ml) lukewarm water (105° to
110°F/40.5° to 43°C)
1½ teaspoons active dry yeast
2¼ cups (315 g) unbleached all-purpose
(plain) flour
4¼ cups (600 g) bread flour
2 teaspoons salt
Cornmeal

1. In a small bowl or glass measuring cup, combine the molasses and water. Sprinkle the yeast over the surface and set aside for 5 to 10 minutes, until the mixture bubbles and foams. Pour the yeast mixture into the bowl of an electric mixer fitted with a dough hook.

2. Add the flours and salt all at once to the bowl and mix on low speed until the flour is incorporated. Increase the speed to medium and knead for 8 minutes, until the dough holds together.

3. Transfer the bowl to a lightly oiled glass or ceramic bowl and cover with plastic wrap (cling film). Let the dough rise in a warm place for about 45 minutes, until doubled in size.

4. Punch down the dough, turn out onto a lightly floured surface, and divide into 2 balls. Knead each ball for 4 to 6 minutes, until the dough tightens. Form the pieces of dough into flattened rounds and set them on a baking sheet sprinkled with cornmeal. Set aside to rise in a warm place for about 30 minutes, until nearly doubled.

5. Meanwhile, position a rack in the center of the oven and a rack below it. Place a large baking stone on the center rack and preheat the oven to 400°F (200°C). Bring a teakettle of water to a boil.

6. Slide the loaves onto the baking stone. Pour boiling water into a roasting pan or large baking dish set on the bottom rack of the oven. Bake for about 35 minutes, until browned and the bottom of the loaves sound hollow when tapped. Cool completely on wire racks.

MAKES TWO 5- TO 6-INCH (13- TO 15-CM) ROUND LOAVES

Note: The hot baking stone and the boiling water in the oven ensure a flaky crust. Be sure the water is boiling when poured into the pan.

GLOSSARY

Al dente An Italian term that translates as "to the tooth" and refers to the degree to which food, usually pasta, is cooked. When food is cooked until al dente, it has been cooked until tender but still offers some resistance when bitten.

Arborio rice A medium-grain white rice grown most widely in northern Italy and used in any number of rice dishes, most notably risotto. The rice contains a high level of amylopectin, a starch that makes the rice creamy. However, the firm inner core of the grain stays intact to the point that it is pleasantly distinctive. *Also see* Carnaroli rice *and* Risotto.

Arrosto A roast of meat.

Arugula A dark-hued green with a strong, sharp, peppery flavor, also known as rocket and rucola. Available from greengrocers, in Italian markets, and in specialty shops, as well as in many supermarkets.

Balsamic vinegar A specialty vinegar that traditionally is made in Modena from white grapes. The best balsamic vinegars are aged for years in wooden barrels and are thick and sweet, with full flavor.

Broccoli rabe A flavorful leafy green with a long stalk and broccoli-like flowers; also known as broccoli rape or raab.

Bruschetta An open-faced sandwich made on warm grilled or toasted peasant-style bread and topped most often with a simple mixture of fresh vegetables. The word is derived from the Italian, *bruscare*, which means to "roast over coals." The most basic bruschetta is made by rubbing fresh garlic over the grilled bread and then sprinkling it with olive oil, salt, and pepper.

Bucatini Long, hollow strand pasta, also called *perciatelli*.

Calamari The Italian word for squid.

Carnaroli rice A medium-grain rice that is grown throughout northern Italy and exported for use in Italian rice dishes, most notably risotto. Available in specialty stores and Italian markets. *Also see* Arborio rice *and* Risotto.

Cavatelli Small, elongated, oval-shaped pasta. Substitute small shells.

Chiffonade A way to prepare greens so that they are cut into thin strips. This is most easily accomplished by rolling the leaves of the green (such as lettuce) into cylinders and slicing them crosswise.

Extra-virgin olive oil The oil from the first pressing of the olives, tasting very strongly of olives. It is best for uncooked preparations such as salad dressings.

Fagioli Defined as "bean" in Italian and most often refers to white navy, cannellini, or kidney beans.

Fontina The best fontina cheese comes from the Alpine region of Italy bordering France and Switzerland and is called Fontina Val d'Aosta. It is a semisoft cow's milk cheese with a mild, nutty flavor and excellent melting properties.

Insalata The Italian word for salad.

Julienne Term for food, usually vegetables, that is cut into narrow uniform strips about the size of matchsticks and an inch long.

Juniper berries Berries with a sweet, piney flavor from the juniper bush. The berries are generally sold dried and classically are used to flavor sauces for strong-tasting meat such as venison and lamb. The world's finest juniper berries are harvested in the Italian Alps.

Kalamata olives Brine-cured purple-to-black Greek olives.

Mascarpone A very soft, rich, and slightly sweet cow's milk cheese usually used in dessert preparations.

Mesclun A mixture of young, tender greens and leafy herbs. Originally made from wild greens, most mesclun mixtures now contain baby lettuces and other cultivated greens.

Mozzarella The best mozzarella cheese is made from the milk of water buffalo and called, appropriately, buffalo mozzarella. Most mozzarella that is locally available is made from cow's milk and is mild, with good melting properties. If you can find handmade fresh mozzarella in an Italian market or specialty shop, it's worth the price.

Olive oil The Italians prefer olive oil over butter and other oils. For cooked preparations, use a high-quality pure olive oil rather than extra-virgin olive oil. *Also see* Extra-virgin olive oil.

Orzo Tiny rice-shaped pasta often used in soups and salads.

Paillard Boneless meat that is pounded very thin.

Pancetta A full-flavored, salt-cured, unsmoked Italian bacon.

Panettone Dome-shaped Italian fruit cake studded with candied fruit peel and raisins.

Pappardelle At 1 inch (2.5 cm) wide, the broadest pasta noodle.

Parmigiano-reggiano Without question, the best Parmesan cheese available in Italy. A grainy, hard, dry cow's milk cheese that is excellent for grating, it is produced in a region mainly comprised of the provinces of Parma and Reggio Emilia in Italy. To be authentic, the rind must be stamped with its name.

Pecorino-romano Hard, grainy, aged sheep's milk cheese meant for grating. This salty, pungent cheese can be used in place of Parmesan.

Penne Short tube-shaped pasta cut at either end on the diagonal, sturdy enough to stand up to nearly all sauces. Also good in salads.

Pennette Small tube-shaped pasta, about half the size of penne.

Pine nuts Small oval-shaped nuts, called *pinoli* or *pignoli* in Italy, which come from the cones of certain pine trees.

Polenta A traditional dish throughout Italy, similar to American cornmeal mush, that may be served warm, at room temperature, or cold. In Roman times polenta was made from grains such as millet, barley, and spelt. Now it is always made from cornmeal.

Porcini mushrooms Wild mushrooms that can weigh less than an ounce (30 g) or more than a pound (450 g). Meaty, with a mild flavor. Also known as cepes, they are often sold dried.

Portobello mushrooms When small, these mushrooms are called cremini, but when they grow large, they are portobellos, favored for their firm, meaty texture.

Prosciutto Aged salt-cured ham that is air-dried for a dense texture and sweet flavor. Parma ham is the best-known prosciutto.

Prosecco Italian sparkling wine. Substitute champagne or a domestic sparkling wine.

Ragu The Italian word for both meat sauce and stew.

Ricotta A fresh Italian cheese made from the whey of various other cheeses. Ricotta is creamy and smooth; dry ricotta is firmer than that sold in most markets and is available only in specialty shops and some Italian markets. You can make an acceptable substitute by letting fresh ricotta drain through cheesecloth for 4 to 8 hours.

Rigatoni Short, hollow, tube-shaped pasta with ridges, especially good with meat sauces and other hearty sauces.

Risotto A creamy, rich rice dish, found throughout northern Italy, that is made by slowly stirring hot liquid (such as chicken stock) into sautéed medium-grain rice. Any number of other ingredients may be added, such as mushrooms, cheese, meats, and shellfish.

Robiola cheese Produced mainly in Piedmont and Lombardy, this soft, slightly tangy and buttery cheese is usually made from cow's milk, although some special versions are made with ewe's milk. Sometimes difficult to locate outside Italy. Substitute dry ricotta if necessary.

Roux A cooked mixture of fat (oil or butter) and flour used to thicken sauces and soups.

Spaghettini Long, thin, stranded cylindrical pasta that is thinner than spaghetti; best with light sauces.

Sun-dried tomatoes Dehydrated tomatoes packed either in olive oil or loose-packed with intense flavor and a chewy texture. Loose-packed tomatoes need to be soaked in warm water to cover for 15 to 20 minutes before they are drained and used in a recipe. Oil-packed tomatoes should be rinsed well under warm water.

Taleggio A triple-cream, semi-soft, smooth farmhouse cheese with a rich, buttery flavor. Similar cheeses include stracchino and crescenza. Substitute Brie or Camembert.

Tubettini Short, tubular pasta.

Tuscan bread A peasant-style, rounded loaf with a chewy crust and firm yet light interior. Popular for sandwiches and bruschetta. Tuscan bread is the peasant-style bread made in Tuscany.

Wonton wrappers Very thin dough squares or rounds used to make Asian dumplings and other preparations with savory fillings. They can be used in place of fresh pasta sheets to make ravioli. Available in most supermarkets and Asian markets.

Zest The colored part of the rind of citrus fruit (usually lemons, oranges, and limes). Especially flavorful and used to flavor and garnish savory and sweet dishes alike. The white pith just below the colored rind is bitter and should be avoided. Use a tool called a zester, a vegetable peeler, or a small sharp knife to cut zest from the fruit.

Zucchini blossoms Edible yellow blossoms that, when in season, are used in any number of Italian dishes as much for their charm as for their mild flavor. Available from specialty greengrocers and Italian markets.

INDEX

(Page numbers in *italic* refer to illustrations.)